A LENTEN PILGRIMAGE —
DYING AND RISING
IN THE LORD

by Richard W. Chilson C.S.P.

Paulist Press
New York/Ramsey

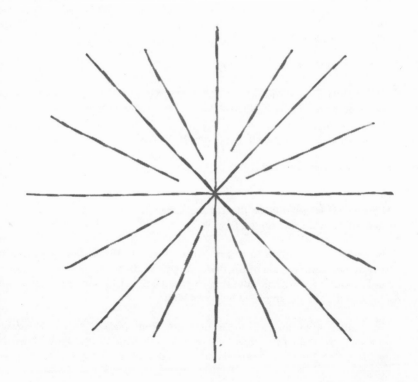

Imprimatur:
Most Reverend John S. Cummins, D.D.
Bishop of Oakland
August 18, 1983

Library of Congress
Catalog Card Number: 83-62520

ISBN: 0-8091-2569-2

Published by Paulist Press
545 Island Road, Ramsey, N.J. 07446

Printed and bound in the United States of America

Book design by Emil Antonucci

Acknowledgements
The English translation of the Nicene Creed is used by permission of the International Consultation on English Texts.

The Scripture quotations in this publication (except the psalms) are from the Revised Standard Version of the Bible, copyrighted 1946, 1952 © 1971, 1973 by the Division of Christian Education of the National Council of Churches of Christ in the U.S.A., and used by permission.

The psalms used in this publication are from *Psalms, A New Translation,* published by William Collins Sons & Co., Ltd. and Paulist Press. Used by permission of The Grail, England and the publishers.

To Brian,
wherever his journey may take him.

CONTENTS

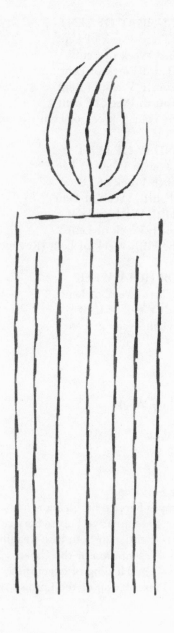

Chapter One

AN INVITATION TO INITIATION

During your recent past you have been embarked upon a conscious journey toward faith. At some time in the past you realized an attraction toward Jesus and his vision. As that attraction deepened you came to the Christian community and enrolled as a catechumen. Through contact with the community, through study, prayer and service, your knowledge of Jesus and of Christianity has grown. You now have a solid grounding in the faith. Of course you will continue to learn and grow as a Catholic. But now a new stage awaits you in your faith journey.

We have described only the outward marks of your journey. In a sense these are secondary to the inward marks which vary greatly from one person to another. We have come to understand faith not simply as a body of knowledge but above all as a relationship with the living God. Our faith itself is a gift from God—a call to enter into intimacy with him in order to grow in his love and wisdom.

Take a moment now to recollect your own journey. Perhaps in the beginning you saw your search as something you were doing. But from your present vantage point can you see that your journey might have truly been a response to God's call? And can you now perceive that same call inviting you to continue your pilgrimage by approaching the sacraments of Christian initiation this Easter?

When we speak of a call from God we need to be aware that we are stretching ordinary language. Such a stretching occurs whenever we speak of God, so far is he beyond our human comprehension. Few of us experience this call as dramatic or unambiguous; St. Paul, knocked off his horse, is the exception rather than the rule. No, for us the call might take the form of a simple attraction and love for Jesus and his

Church. It might come to us from a person we love. It could be as ordinary as feeling at home in this Christian community. But there is more here than our love, our desire, our feeling at home; through these experiences and feelings God is calling us to himself.

We are now approaching a time for decision. Our pilgrimage is not an automatic progression. There are times for re-evaluation and a deepening of commitment. How do you feel at this time about becoming a Catholic Christian? Are you ready for initiation at this time? You have been exploring your own journey with many people through the catechumenate—with your fellow catechumens, with your sponsor, with the catechists and ministers. They can help you now through discussion and prayer to discern whether you are being called by God. What difficulties or obstacles have been overcome for you? What problems remain today? What are the things calling you to complete your journey?

Since your decision is important and concerns a deep commitment to Jesus and his Church, it cannot and should not be rushed or pressured. It is not dictated by what classes you have attended or what timetable you have fulfilled. You are being called by God to a decision to follow him by becoming a Catholic Christian. It is a mystery between you and God which unravels in the depths of your being. As you pray over it and share your feelings and thoughts with others you will be able to clarify what is happening. If you feel called to baptism or Catholic membership, and if your sponsors and teachers concur in your decision, then at the beginning of Lent your pilgrimage will enter upon a new level.

On the first Sunday of Lent we will celebrate together your election by God for Christian initiation. During the course of this Lent you will prepare yourself through prayer, fasting and penance. You will be joined in these actions by the other candidates as well as by the entire Christian community. For we are here to support you on your journey, and you, for your part, renew our faith through your own coming to faith.

Perhaps you are already a baptized Christian. For you this journey is a deepening and expansion of your Christianity through your exploration of the Catholic Church. While you do not have necessarily the same experience as the person encountering Jesus for the first time, still your change of church membership provides an opportunity to re-examine your faith and move toward a deeper commitment to and conversion toward Jesus. Conversion for the Christian is not a one-time action. Conversion is ongoing throughout our life. Each Lent the entire community joins with the elect in examining their lives and turning ever more fully toward the Lord. This Lent as you prepare for membership in the Catholic Church you are called by God to use this occasion as a time of renewal and rededication to Jesus. So although this book and the Lenten celebrations speak most directly to those preparing for baptism, all Christians, and especially you preparing to become Catholics, can use it to nurture your ongoing conversion.

This manual is meant to assist you in your Lenten pilgrimage. It fits into and helps prepare you for the various prayers and rituals celebrated throughout the Lenten season. In addition it provides you with a short prayer time each day (about ten minutes) that will help you bring into your concrete daily life what we are celebrating in church. This is a book to use, not merely to read. It is not an end in itself but only an aid for your journey. Of course there will be days or even periods when you might not be able or willing to use it—that is to be expected. But if you should miss a day or so, try to renew your commitment and return to your prayer. This Lenten preparation is most important for you—it will set the foundations for your baptism and your subsequent Christian life.

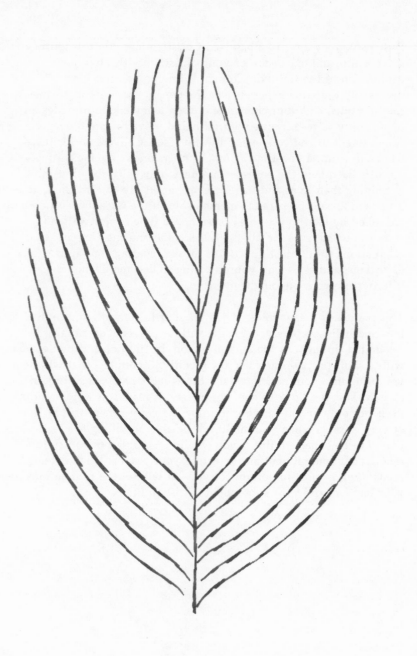

Chapter Two

THE MEANING OF LENT

The word "Lent" derives from the Anglo-Saxon "lencten" which means "spring." Now although Lent does occur in springtime it is hardly the Christian festival of spring—that is, Easter. For Christians Lent has developed as a time of preparation for Easter—a spiritual spring cleaning that prepares us to celebrate Jesus' victory over sin and death.

Over the centuries the common Christian practice and understanding of Lent has changed greatly. Lent became a time of penitence; Christians recalled the sufferings of Jesus and did penance in sorrow for their sins. The Lenten fast which in former times was much more strict than today ensured Lent a more prominent place in people's experience than Easter. But Lent is only the preparation for Easter. Furthermore some ideas of fasting and penance appeared negative and life-denying to many people. Were we not merely beating ourselves for not being as good as we thought we should be? With all these distortions Lent lost much of its original purpose.

Yet there were advantages to Lent as well. Christianity tells us of a possibility of transformation, yet that is not possible without discipline, and Lent provides just that. Our fast was also an opportunity for cleansing. Once a year we drew back from our habitual models of living, and through our fasting we purified and cleansed ourselves of poisons and habits which had simply become a part of us. And finally our communal experience of fasting and praying provided a sense of solidarity throughout the Catholic community; we were in this fast together as we came to feel the support and challenge of undertaking this communal penance.

The Second Vatican Council in its restoration of the liturgy addressed the question of Lent so that its true purpose might once more be understood and appreciated.

The season of Lent has a twofold character: primarily by recalling or preparing for baptism and by penance, it disposes the faithful, who more diligently hear the word of God and devote themselves to prayer, to celebrate the paschal mystery (Constitution on the Sacred Liturgy 109).

At Easter new people are born into the Christian community through baptism which powerfully makes present for us the death and resurrection of Jesus. So Lent first of all prepares the elect for their baptism and initiation. For this reason the Sunday Scriptures speak on the themes of suffering and death, of rebirth and renewal. We shall explore the symbols surrounding the sacraments as we pray and celebrate together this Lent. We will come to see how these symbols speak of God and his love for us. We will learn how these symbols have been present in all human culture, how they were taken up into Israel's history to reveal God to his people, how they became part of Jesus' life as he opened his disciples to their deeper significance. Gradually we will be led to the pool of baptism where these same symbols will reveal for us the depths and riches of life and growth in Christ.

But Lent is not only for the elect. At Easter all Christians recall their own baptism and celebrate God's redeeming love which leads us out of our darkness and into the light of Christ's Kingdom. So in a sense all Christians join with the elect on this pilgrimage of prayer and penance so that at Easter as we witness these baptisms we might come to a deeper appreciation and understanding of our own baptism. For although this sacrament is given only once it does not disappear or cease working once the action is over. All through our life we continue to explore what God has done for us in this mystery. And as we open ourselves more to our Father we allow him to lead us further into the new life he prepares for us.

The second character of Lent is penitential. As the Second Vatican Council explained,

By penance (Lent) ... disposes the faithful, who more diligently hear the word of God and devote themselves to prayer, to celebrate the paschal mystery (Constitution on the Sacred Liturgy 109).

But Lenten penance provides difficulty today to many Christians. For our common understanding of penance is quite different from that of Jesus and the early Church. It is this wholesome notion of penance that we must recover if our keeping of Lent is to bear fruit.

The Nature of Penance

Penance is necessary in the first place because we are all caught in the bondage of sin. Jesus showed us a new way of living and seeing life by means of his parables and signs. Instead of continuing to live as we have learned to do, he invites us to share with him the vision appropriate to the Kingdom of God. We have glimpsed that Kingdom through Jesus. Our decision to follow him by becoming a Christian is a decision to move from our present ties to worldly thought and action into a life inspired by God and his Kingdom. We have decided to give up a way of living that puts our own will first; with Jesus we now want to pray, "Thy will be done."

But such a switch in allegiance is not that easy. The truth is that we are stuck in our old ways. Deciding to act differently will not make it so. We have been thinking and acting in this way for years. Such ingrained habits are hard to change; indeed they are even hard to recognize as habits rather than as simply the way things are. What makes us believe that our will so used to its own way will gladly surrender its powers to another, even if that other is God?

Jesus is quite clear about the cost of following him, "If any man would come after me, let him deny himself and take up his cross and follow me" (Mt 16:24). To follow Jesus we will have to deny ourselves. We will have to say no to that part of us that wants to be in the center. Only through this denial can we become selfless. And only by being selfless can there be room for the Father and his Kingdom to come into our life.

Self-denial is not very popular in our culture or even among many Christians today. We are very comfortable and rather indulgent people, and this accounts for some of the reaction against penance. But some reaction is against a false and unhealthy self-denial. Too often self-denial has been used as a way of expressing and fostering self-hatred and neurotic feelings of meekness and humility. People have scourged their bodies, believing that the flesh is evil and to be scorned. They have denied themselves as a way of heaping contempt upon themselves. But these kinds of self-denial are not what Jesus calls us to.

For Christians self-denial is a means of discipline—a method for learning how to live selflessly. We do not hate the flesh; how can we hate that which God became? We do not despise ourselves. Through our self-denial we can tame ourselves, realign our priorities according to the vision of the Kingdom, and so achieve some of the true happiness which Jesus has promised us.

Carl Jung, the great psychologist, can provide us with a model of what we are trying to achieve through our self-denial. Jung sees us as fragmented people. There is an ego—an "I"—which likes to think that it is in charge of us, even that it is all of us. But there is more to us than merely the ego. For one thing there is what Jung called the shadow. Here lie parts of our being which we attempt to deny. Often we project onto other people these qualities that we cannot abide in ourselves. But this projection does us little real good. Instead Jung sees the way to health through a greater integration of our total self. We need to come to a knowledge of our own shadow side. And we need to reconcile ourselves with the shadow and the other parts of ourselves. Only this reconciliation will bring us true peace and happiness. So then our work of self-denial places conflict in our life which in turn throws light on our shadow side. We come to see in ourselves those qualities we project onto others. And once we come to see these split-off fragments of ourself we can move with God's help toward reconciliation and integration.

In addition our self-denial brings to our attention the plight of our brothers and sisters throughout the world who daily are denied even the necessities of life. Through our penance we come to share in their situation. We come to feel solidarity with the poor and oppressed. Our penance raises our consciousness and creates compassion. And that compassion brings us to join with the poor in their struggle so that they too might come to share in the bounties of our Father's world.

We know as well that much of the oppression in our world is caused by our own blindness. Our penance can reveal to us the extent to which we and our nation create oppression. Then we might move to break the oppression at its source and make reparation to those who have suffered for so long. We follow Jesus in the hope of entering his Kingdom. But how can that Kingdom where all shall live in wholeness come about as long as even we are working against it by denying the benefits of God's goodness to our sisters and brothers who share this earth with us?

Repentance

We can arrive at a deeper understanding of penance by considering some of the words used by Christians to speak of it; let us consider conversion, metanoia and repentance. Each of these words focuses upon a different center in our being. For conversion or turning toward God is really a matter of the heart. Metanoia on the other hand refers more to the mind—change your mind, change your accustomed ways of thinking. And repentance could refer to our body or our will—what we do, how we act. By looking more closely at these centers of heart, mind and will we can gain a more complete picture of penance.

We begin with the will, for it is here that we can see the results. Often people believe that repentance is somewhat like being sorry.

We have done something wrong; we have hurt someone and so we repent—we feel sorrow for what we have done and try to rectify the wrong. Now while this is one meaning of repentance it is not the most profound meaning. Repentance is not simply putting bandages on the wounds we have caused. For what good would such repentance really do? Yes, it is valuable in the current situation. But will such repentance help us refrain from hurting someone in the future? Will it enable us to live more by the vision of God's Kingdom? Hardly.

The difference between the way we live and perceive things (which Jesus calls the world) and the way of seeing which belongs to the Kingdom is great indeed. More than sorrow is needed to move us from our current attitudes and vision into those of the Kingdom. All the bandages in the world will not really bring us close. It is our attitudes, our thoughts which brought us into that sinful action in the first place that must be repented of. The real problem is not the hateful words we speak in anger which hurt our friend. The real problem is the fears and insecurities we fell into which led us into hateful words.

In true repentance we try to move behind all of our sins to the sinful condition itself. What makes us act to hurt people? What prevents us from forgiving others? Why are we afraid to love?

In the Zen Buddhist tradition a pupil who wishes to move toward enlightenment is sometimes given a riddle to solve. This riddle or koan does not make ordinary sense. The pupil must wrestle with it daily over a period of time until finally he or she surrenders his or her reason. Only then can the answer to the koan be grasped by the mind. A famous koan can help us comprehend the depth of repentance needed for us to enter the Kingdom way of life: "What is the shape of your original face before you were conceived?" Certainly such a question seems ridiculous on the surface. We had no face before we were conceived. Yet let us not give up so easily. Before we were conceived we could say we existed in the mind of

God. And our existence there is our true existence—who we truly are, how we truly look. But then we were conceived in our mother's womb. We were born into the human race with its warped view of the way things are. No longer could we see our original face. The face we see now is not how we truly are in God's mind. Rather it shows what we have become in the world's mind if indeed it has one.

But through repentance can we not make that journey back to the mind of God to discover how we truly are? This is our journey and our task. We are not concerned so much with healing the various wounds we have acquired or inflicted. We want to move to the heart of the matter; we want to discover our integrated self as it was and as it still is in the mind of God. For if we can discover who we truly are then we shall naturally be able to act in accordance with our original face. Then it won't be a problem of avoiding sin—by nature we shall act in a wholesome and healthy way.

Conversion

Our second word for penance—conversion—takes us into the realm of the heart. As St. Paul said, we know what is right and what is wrong but that does not do us any good. Neither Paul nor we can prevent ourselves from doing what is wrong and failing to do the good. It does not help to know; we can read all the books of wisdom but they will not necessarily help us to do the good. But there is a way out of this prison. And, as Paul proclaims, that way is Jesus Christ who, while we were still in sin, died for us so that we might be brought out of our sin and into our Father's love.

In the area of the heart love conquers all. Certainly if we are able to turn our heart toward God we would find a way out of our prison. And the good news is that Jesus manifests God's love for us, even to the point of dying for us. We are already reconciled in him. In truth there is nothing remaining to be set aright. All that remains now is for us to recognize this great love and allow it to renew us. When we allow God to love us and enter our heart we find ourselves recreated. In Jesus God has taken upon himself our likeness out of love. When we acknowledge his love we take on the image of God which we discover in Jesus. We once more come to resemble our original face.

Conversion has always been just this call to a real change of heart. The prophets called Israel to conversion: It is not your sacrifices and your rituals or other religious practices that I desire. Rather let your heart be turned toward me. Open your heart to the poor in the land so that you cease your exploitation and oppression. Let me remove your hearts of stone and replace them with hearts of flesh.

Similarly in our own conversion the external actions are not the core of the matter. Externals are only important if they are in harmony with our internal life. If they are not, we are mere hypocrites, saying and celebrating one thing but living another. And how might we allow this conversion to occur? We might begin by simply listening to what God has already accomplished for us in his love. We are being wooed by God in Jesus. He wishes to be with us, to heal us, to forgive us, to love us, to raise us from death into life. As we open ourselves to God's plan for us we may gradually fall in love as well—first with ourselves to heal the division within us, then with God and with all his creation.

And things begin to happen when we fall in love. The world changes. You are no longer the same. You begin to see things through the eyes of your beloved. You want to be like your beloved. You want to join in union with the beloved. Nor is this attempt at union hard or difficult. You want to do it. You cannot be content until you share everything in union with your love.

Metanoia

When we consider what separates us from union with God we find that it is our worldly vision and attitude. In Matthew's Gospel when Jesus announces that he must go to Jerusalem, there to be handed over and killed, Simon Peter protests that he should do no such thing. Jesus' reply (Mt 16:23) seems quite harsh. He says (to use my own translation), "Get behind me, Satan! You see not as God sees but as the world sees." The word "Satan" might give us pause. Jesus is not really calling Peter the devil as we popularly understand that word. That would be strange indeed since Jesus has just put Peter in authority over the Church. Here Satan is a symbol for that part of the world in antagonism to God. It is not the world that is evil; no, the world is God's creation and by nature good. But things are out of joint in the world. Worldly values are not the values of the Kingdom. Satan relies upon power and force rather than love. Satan counsels harshness and retaliation rather than forgiveness. Satan believes in "me first" rather than in charity and generosity. Satan believes in saving your own skin rather than saving the world. The whole of humanity including most Christians shares in these ideas and values; it is this spirit which Jesus rebukes in Peter: Peter, you are thinking and seeing as the spirit of this world has taught you. Do not cling to these ideas. Instead begin to see life as it truly is when seen in the light of my Father's Kingdom.

If we would leave the tyranny of Satan behind it is necessary that we change our vision, our outlook, our attitudes, our grounding beliefs. We are called to metanoia—to change our minds. For it is our basic belief structures that create and foment all the sinful acts which pollute our world. If we can move out of these beliefs, putting in their place the values of the Kingdom, we will find our life and our world changing.

Just what are these basic beliefs? We can begin with something as fundamental to human existence as fear and worry. Every one of us is caught in webs of anxiety. Think how much time you devote to these "realities." Yet what does Jesus say concerning them? Throughout the Scriptures the advice is to fear not. Yes, there is a value to fear. When we are in a dangerous situation our fear alerts us to the danger and hopefully marshals our resources to deal with the problem. But fear and worry consume much more of our time than just such emergency situations. Our fear is generalized and tinges all of our living. Indeed as Jesus points out, our worry can prevent us from living altogether. So Jesus encourages us not to worry. What does all this worry gain us? Nothing. Since it does no good let us drop it. Do not worry about what tomorrow may bring. Each day has troubles of its own.

But is Jesus' teaching trustworthy? Can worry really be that useless? Am I truly wasting my time with worry? It must serve some purpose. Yet we are attracted to Jesus' teaching at the same time. Who of us would not have our lives significantly improved if we were able to drop our fear and worry?

But it is much easier said than done—this dropping of worry and other worldly beliefs. When we explore the extent of worry in our own life we find just how deeply ingrained, how much a part of us, how terribly natural it has become. As we try to let go of these ideas and habits we often find ourselves even more deeply embedded in them. They have become so much a part of us that we are blind to their importance and presence in our life. Only when we begin to examine them and work with them do we come to realize how extensive a hold they have on us.

We were, to use modern language, brainwashed into these beliefs and attitudes. But the situation is more serious still. There is a part of us—indeed it would like us to think of it as the whole of us— which is quite committed to keeping us stuck in the ways of the world, in the ideology of Satan. We can call this part of us by various names. Carl Jung speaks of it as the ego. It is the part which when we say "I" forms the center of us. It is that part of us that uses fear and worry to keep itself in power. It is that part of us that claims to love but really only wants to control and possess the beloved. When wronged, it seeks only vengeance and backs away from forgiveness. It stands between our enslavement to Satan and our liberation as God's children.

Chapter Three

OUR LENTEN PRACTICE

The penance we undertake for Lent helps unmask the worldly attitude which contaminates us. Our penance creates conflict in our life. That conflict wakes us up to things which were previously unconscious. Our ego does not like the conflict and attempts to win us back to its own ways of thinking. But, like Jesus in the wilderness, we can listen to these voices of ego and distance ourself from them. Instead of allowing the ego to continue to be our all, through the conflict and what we discover we can back off from the ego's tyranny and allow all the different aspects of ourself to emerge. In addition, the conflict places us in a very difficult situation. We cannot win this conflict on our own. But through the struggle we can learn to rely more upon God. Through our experience we can discover the power of God to bring us through temptation and make us whole.

Lenten Fast

There are many possibilities for Lenten penance. The most common practice has been the Lenten fast. In denying our bodies food we are pushed back upon God for sustenance. We learn that physical food does not ultimately sustain us or make our life full.

By fasting we also come to share in the experience of the poor and hungry of the world. As we share in their experience we come to feel solidarity with them—the poor become a part of our world, they become our brothers and sisters. We awaken to their needs and troubles and hopefully come to join with them in their struggle for liberation.

There are certain days during Lent when all Catholics fast and abstain from meat. These days are Ash Wednesday, at the very beginning of Lent, and Good Friday, the day Jesus died. In addition many Catholics, depending on the regulations of the individual diocese, abstain from meat on the Fridays of Lent in memory of Jesus' sufferings and death. We abstain together on these days as a sign of our repentance and our desire to turn toward God and his Kingdom.

Fasting has a specific definition in Roman Catholic practice. The rules on fasting define the minimum necessary to observe the fast; many people observe far more than the minimum. On a day of fast we eat one normal meal during the day—usually supper. In addition we may eat two other meals which, combined, do not exceed the main meal. Of course we do not eat between meals on such days. All Catholics over the age of fourteen are bound by the laws of abstinence. The regulations on fasting apply to Catholics between the ages of twenty-one and fifty-nine.

For our extended Lenten practice we may choose some form of fast. However any prolonged period of rigorous fasting (the Catholic fast is not rigorous) should be supervised by a physician as there are possible dangers.

Other Forms of Penance

But there are other forms of penance as well. Jesus encouraged and practiced almsgiving and the vigil as ways of working upon oneself. Through almsgiving we aid the poor directly. And our practice of giving away some of our money may raise issues of money in our life. How is our money spent? What importance does money truly hold for us? It is all too easy for us to make money into a kind of god. Almsgiving helps us put money in its proper place. The practice of the vigil helps us do the same thing with sleep and prayer. In a vigil we spend the night praying rather than sleeping.

Of course the penance you choose should touch some issues in your life which you would like to explore. During Lent many Christians examine habits which have formed and which may call for some attention; smoking is only one of the most popular. Look at your life: is there some habit you would like to bring under control? Perhaps you drink more than you feel good about. You might abstain from alcohol either with the idea of giving it up altogether or simply to enable you to re-examine its place in your life. Perhaps you notice that you are stingy with your money, your time, your possessions. You might work on that attitude by choosing to give some money or time each week (whatever will slightly inconvenience you and bring the issue to the fore) to a charity so that others might be helped.

Other people are uncomfortable with the negative image of giving up for Lent. Instead they develop something that has been missing from their life. Maybe you have been thinking about meditating or jogging or doing something beneficial for a long time. You might visit sick parishioners in the hospital; you might do some volunteer work for the community. Lent is an excellent moment to begin. We have over forty days of discipline ahead of us in which all Christians will strive to come closer to the Kingdom. What better opportunity to undertake something new with all this good will, support and community around us?

Take some time before Lent begins to decide upon your own practice. You might discuss it with your sponsor, with the other catechumens, or with your spouse or family. You might undertake a penance in union with others. The members of the group can then provide support and encouragement to all.

Some Guidelines

When you have settled upon a practice, examine it by means of the following guidelines. All too often people begin Lent with the best intentions but become casualties along the way. If we can prevent these failures before they happen we can ensure ourselves a better experience of Lent.

First ask whether you *really* want to do this penance. Often we choose something that we convince ourselves we *should* do. And perhaps indeed we should do it. But the real question is whether at this point we are ready and want to do it. It may be true that you smoke too much. But until you are ready and want to stop or cut down you are almost certainly setting up a failure. If it is possible, ask yourself this question about your practice on at least two different occasions before Lent begins. Ask yourself when you feel enthusiastic. But ask yourself as well when you are not on top of the world and filled with enthusiasm.

The second question to consider is how much conflict this penance will create in your life. A penance that creates no conflict is not much of a tool for transformation. It will not bring you to trust more in God. It will not unmask the voice of ego for you. It will be quite easy, and, being easy, of not much use as a penance no matter how beneficial in other ways.

Of course the other extreme is no good either. If the penance creates a great amount of conflict you will make yourself miserable. And the more miserable you are the harder it will be to persevere. We want a penance that creates conflict in our life but that will not overly disrupt it. The penance should help us grow in our trust in God. As we build that trust over the years we will be enabled to undertake greater tasks. But it does little good to throw ourselves into the fire right away; all we do then is guarantee failure.

Finally let us ask how the penance we have chosen for ourselves might bring us close to God. Will it awaken us to the resources available to us in prayer? Will it open our eyes to our own selfishness and draw us out of it? How do we see this Lenten practice moving us closer to and preparing us for our baptism at Easter—our dying and rising in the Lord? Is our penance a practice of dying in some way? If it is, then by our dying we shall give God the opportunity to raise us up.

Once you have considered these questions in relation to your chosen practice ask yourself again whether you still choose this as your practice. If you do then write a brief contract with yourself and God. Specify exactly what you are committing yourself to. Mention all the exceptions and conditions you foresee arising. Spell it all out. And in conclusion compose a short prayer asking God to help you persevere and grow through your penance. During Lent whenever you are tempted to abandon or modify your original intention you can return to this contract and this prayer to find strength and resolve.

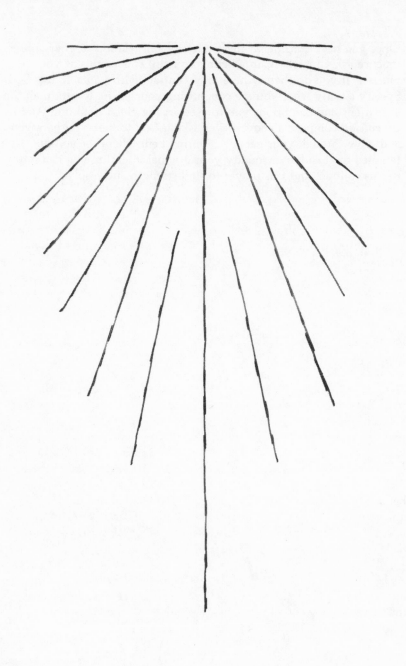

Chapter Four

OUR LENTEN PRAYER

This Lent is a time for serious praying and looking at our life in preparation for our baptism and reception into the Catholic community this Easter. There are various forms this prayer takes. Each Sunday during the course of Lent you will be participating in various rituals during the Sunday liturgies together with the other elect. In addition you will be gathering together once a week for community prayer. But this prayer with the other members of your group and the Christian community is grounded in and supported by your individual prayer. This prayerbook is designed to guide you on your individual prayer journey by complementing and deepening what happens on Sundays and at the weekly prayer meetings.

Each day we will be praying for ten to fifteen minutes. This is not a long period of time—we waste much more time in the course of a normal day. Yet you will discover in prayer a real source of growth and nourishment for your journey toward Easter. To support your prayer take time now to decide on a good time for prayer each day. For if we have an appointed time we are less likely to leave the prayer until we have time—which often leads to no time for prayer. Choose as well a place for your prayer where you can be quiet and undisturbed. The place need only be a corner of some room, but make it comfortable and attractive so that you will come to enjoy being there and in prayer. You can help create a prayerful atmosphere by means of a holy picture, a candle, incense, or even a flower—all this can help us enter into prayer. In addition you will need only a Bible and this prayerbook.

As you begin each day's prayer take a moment to become quiet and leave behind your ordinary cares and concerns. Next read through the Scripture text for the day's prayer if there is one. Then read through the prayerbook for the day. Once that is done you can go back and actually pray. If you find yourself resisting the prayer remember that this resistance is also part of the prayer experience. Try to discover why you are resisting.

If you miss one or more days try not to scold yourself or chalk it up as a failure. Instead simply return to the practice. One or two days missed will not hurt, and if you are curious you can always go back and read what was missed later. The important thing is to get back into the habit again with as little time lost as possible.

Each week at the prayer meeting you will have an opportunity to share your pilgrimage during the previous week. Each Wednesday's prayer is designed to help us in this evaluation. Thus if your prayer group meets on a day other than Wednesday you should do the Wednesday section of that week on the day of the meeting.

Chapter Five

ASH WEDNESDAY
AND THE FIRST SUNDAY OF LENT

Ash Wednesday

First Sunday of Lent

The Readings: Cycle A — Genesis 2:7 - 9, 3:1 - 7;
Romans 5:12 - 19; Matthew 4:1 - 11
Cycle B — Genesis 9:8 - 15; 1 Peter 3:18 - 22;
Mark 1:12 - 15
Cycle C — Deuteronomy 26:4 - 10; Romans 10:8 - 13;
Luke 4:1 - 13

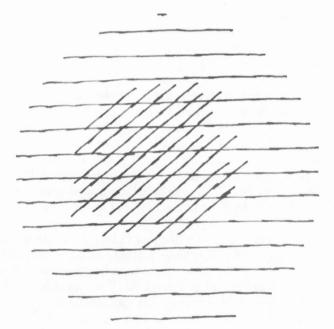

ASH WEDNESDAY

We begin Lent by listening to a call to change our life. It is time to examine our living so that we might discover how far we are from a full life. The ashes distributed today are a sign of the deadness in our life. They remind us that we are indeed dust and shall once more become dust. How easy it is for us to lose sight of this basic reality. We see ourselves as anything but dust. We feel life coursing within us and convince ourselves that we are invincible—we will live forever. We hide our weaknesses from ourselves. We deceive ourselves concerning our imperfections and failings; it wasn't really my fault; I'm only human. And so we try to ignore or even forget the death piling up right now in our life which will eventually overtake us altogether.

But if we do not bring to mind and reflect upon our deaths it becomes impossible for us to live fully. We delude ourselves. We may live constantly for the future forgetting that such a future may never come. We fret about a million little things and lose sight of the truly important issues in our life. When a person is told that he or she has only a short while to live, often his or her way of life changes drastically. There can now be no more putting off till tomorrow. Life must be lived in the now and to the fullest.

By urging us to repent Jesus is calling us to become aware of our deaths. This call should not make us morbid and depressed; rather it can wake us up to the possibility of real life. Consider now those areas of your life that are already dead. Are you still clinging to them as though they were alive? Do they make it difficult for you to go about the business of living? Lent can be a spiritual spring housecleaning. What is lying around your life that is no longer alive, no longer a vital part of you, that you might better discard?

Let us consider as well those aspects of our life that may be dying right now. In becoming Christian we are asking the Lord to transform us. What things are keeping you from the life promised in the Gospel? What in yourself needs to die before you can be raised up in the resurrected life of Easter? When we begin to look at our life in this way we might be tempted to see only the big issues. But let us include the small things as well, for these are the areas where we can begin to repent. How much do we tend to view our happiness in terms of material things and possessions? Does our grasping bring us real satisfaction? Can we begin to loosen our possessions' hold over us? How much of our time is occupied with worry, fear or judgment? Can we begin in little ways to catch ourselves in worry and then surrender that worry to the Lord? Take a few moments to call to mind all the death and dying that is part of your life right now.

Jesus assures us that such death is not an end in itself. Death leads to resurrection if only we allow God to raise us up. So let us take all the death we have discovered in our life and imagine how we might be resurrected from it. All too often we can only see the death when we are in the midst of it. And death can seem so final. But Jesus offers us hope. And we can make that hope our own by daring to imagine some kind of resurrection for ourselves.

To conclude our meditation ask your Father to be with you on your Lenten pilgrimage. Ask him to reveal to you the deaths in your life, to lead you through those deaths so that you may enjoy the light of Easter. Ask that the penance you are undertaking be a means of growth and transformation. Ask for help in doing this penance.

Today is a day of fast and abstinence. The directions for fasting and abstaining are given in chapter three. But there is more to fasting than simply following the rules. Our attitude toward the fast was very important to Jesus. To conclude today read Jesus' instructions for penance and fasting in Matthew 6:1 - 6, 16 - 18.

THURSDAY AFTER ASH WEDNESDAY

Cycle A — Matthew 4:1 - 11
Cycle B — Mark 1:12 - 15
Cycle C — Luke 4:1 - 13

For the first two Sundays of Lent the lessons still follow a three year cycle. In our prayer therefore choose for your reading and meditation the story appropriate to the year. For example if the Church is reading the A Cycle, then you will choose and concentrate only on the A readings. Fortunately there are themes that cut across the cycles in each of these readings, and we shall be concentrating upon these themes in our introductions to prayer here. Your catechists can tell you which cycle the Church is currently in if you do not know.

Our Gospel story today underlines and can give guidance to our own Lenten practice. After his baptism Jesus went into the desert forty days to have his vocation tested. There Satan approaches him and tempts him in three ways.

Although all the Gospels for the three cycles speak of Jesus' temptation today, there are real differences between them. Mark is the briefest. He merely says that Jesus went into the wilderness where he was tempted. Matthew and Luke fill in the story by describing three of the temptations in detail. Now these are not meant to be historical accounts. Each Gospel writer is using the fact of Jesus' sojourn in the desert to develop certain themes. For example the three temptations are modeled upon incidents that occurred when Israel was in the wilderness for forty years after escaping from Egypt. The Gospel writers are showing that whereas Israel proved unfaithful, Jesus was obedient and therefore is the true Israel or child of God. For the purposes of our discussion today we shall rely primarily upon Matthew's account. In your prayer and reflection you might wish to use the account you will hear at this Sunday's liturgy.

Jesus is fasting in the desert. And one of the first symptoms of the fast is great hunger. "If you are the Son of God," suggests Satan, "why don't you turn these stones into bread and feed yourself?" We can sympathize with this temptation from our own experience of fasting. There are many ways we might try to get around the fast. Just a little piece of toast won't break the fast. This little piece of candy doesn't count. During your own fasting and your Lenten practice you have already or will soon hear such voices urging you to compromise in some way.

The Gospel story dramatizes the encounter by speaking of Satan as a person who comes to tempt Jesus. But we could just as easily tell the story as a struggle between Jesus and his own ego. The voice of Satan—the father of lies, as Jesus calls him—speaks within each one of us urging us this way or that. And it is just this dominating voice with which we contend during our Lenten practice. Unfortunately our idea of Satan has become fantastic. We either make him into a cousin of Dracula, or we picture him as some great evil force we would want nothing to do with. In either instance we have lost the original idea of the tempter.

But in our story today we see neither a monster nor some shapeless evil. Instead Satan has a voice much like the voices we hear telling us what to do. And does he tell Jesus to do anything that is so wrong? No. Satan's ideas are quite practical, and they seem to make a good deal of sense as well. First, you are hungry. Isn't it natural that you should eat to satisfy your hunger? What could be wrong with that?

In the second temptation Satan takes Jesus up to the parapet of the temple. "If you are the Son of God, throw yourself off this temple. God will rescue you, and then you can be sure that you really are his beloved." Again ask yourself just what the problem is with this idea. Jesus has had a great revelation at his baptism: he saw the heavens open and heard the voice proclaim him the beloved Son of God. But now it is some time later. He has been in the desert and is weak from the fast. Can he be sure that the vision was true? Did it only seem that way? There certainly doesn't seem to be much consolation in being the Son of God here in this wilderness. Wouldn't it be confirming to have some further proof that such is the case and that he is not simply being deceived? Why not a test such as jumping off the temple?

But Jesus replies that we should not put God to the test. We are called to trust in God rather than to test him. We cannot always be looking for confirmations and assurances. Rather as Jesus shows we must learn to live without such constant revelation. It is enough to trust in God, having faith that we are loved and will be sustained.

The third temptation also appears reasonable. "If you are the Messiah then you should take matters into your own hands and set things right. Listen to me and obey me and I will give you the power to do what you want." Yet Jesus knows that it is not up to him to take matters into his own hands. Instead he worships only God and allows God to determine when and by what means the Kingdom will come.

From this story we might take guidance for our own Lenten practice. Perhaps already we have heard voices telling us to rethink our position. Maybe they hint at our foolishness in undertaking such a practice. Besides who would ever know if we broke our resolution? It isn't that important anyway.

Again and again these temptations will come. But like Jesus, let us recognize them as the work of our own ego—of Satan, if we will. Through this Lenten observance we are separating ourselves from our ego's dominance over us. Obviously our ego will not surrender its power without a great fight. This is what Lent is all about.

But let us take Jesus as our model for Lent. Listen to the voices when they arise. Some will seem quite reasonable; often the suggestion may seem the preferable thing to do. But listen to the voices. See if you can, like Jesus, unmask them and recognize them as temptations. When we are tempted to follow them, then, like Jesus, can we hold to our resolution and surrender ourselves to God to help us through this time of testing? Are there any times already when you have been tested in this way? How did you respond?

In today's prayer ask your Father to help you keep your Lenten resolution. Ask him in times of temptation to help you separate yourself from your ego's domination so that you might be free to serve God by following instead the promptings of the Holy Spirit.

FRIDAY AFTER ASH WEDNESDAY
Cycle A — Genesis 2:7 - 9; 3:1 - 7
Cycle B — Genesis 9:8 - 15
Cycle C — Deuteronomy 26:4 - 10

The Old Testament lessons during Lent recount the history of our salvation. Cycle A begins at the very beginning with the story of Adam and Eve in the garden of Eden. Modern Scripture scholars attempt to understand the Bible as the people who first wrote it understood it. In their studies of these stories today it has been discovered that these stories were not intended to be taken as history (in our modern understanding of the term) but as myth. A myth is a story whose truth resides in its meaning; this story speaks about the human condition—not biological genesis. Nor are the other readings from B and C primarily historical either. They are more concerned with meaning than with what happened or how things happened. And the common theme through all these readings is our relationship with God and his many covenants with us.

The idea of the covenant which expresses our relationship with God is central throughout the Hebrew Scriptures and comes to full flowering for Christians in Jesus. Time and again God has sought us out and tried to enter into relationship with us. The stories here describe three of those attempted covenants.

The first is at the beginning of creation. Adam and Eve are placed in a garden where all their needs will be taken care of. The one demand is that they not eat of the tree of the knowledge of good and evil. But they disobey and eat of the fruit, hoping that in doing so they will become gods.

Could this story describe our own journey from the innocence of childhood (where we did not know of distinctions between good and evil, but simply had to obey our elders) to the situation of adulthood where we know good and evil and life is no longer an innocent garden experience but is filled with confusion, ambiguity and sin? Can we remember our own fall from innocence? Can we not identify with Adam and Eve's longing to become like gods? Is this not at the root of the human dilemma, the cause of much of our pain and sorrow?

In the story of Noah and the flood we see God striking out against the evil of humanity through a terrible destruction. But then we witness a new covenant which God offers—a covenant of reconciliation. God promises never again to strike out with such violence. (We need to remember when we read these stories that they are from a quite primitive culture, whose ideas of God seem quite foreign to us—humanity has grown over the centuries and our concepts of God have evolved as well.)

The most important feature of the story of Noah is this new covenant of the rainbow. Here we begin to catch a glimpse of God— what he is like. Once again he reaches out to us, calls us into relationship with him. Although sin and human evil may have broken the covenant with Adam and Eve, God now offers yet another covenant, another chance for union with him.

Israel's very existence as we see in the reading for Cycle C comes from another covenant. Israel would not exist had God not seen the slaves suffering in Egypt and had compassion for their condition. He delivered them from slavery and brought them into freedom. Israel has no claim to fame except to rejoice in what God has done for her.

In each of these covenants we can discern two themes. First and most important are the blessings of God which he wishes to shower upon us through the covenant: the blessings of the garden, the blessings of the rainbow, the blessings of freedom. And on the other side we must note that humanity has failed each of the covenants. Adam and Eve sinned; all humanity was depraved in Noah's time; Israel would sin over and over again. But in spite of that human frailty, that sinfulness, the blessings of God continue. He tries again and again to enter into relationship with us, to bless us, to make us his own, to bring us freedom.

In the Gospel story for this Sunday we see Jesus as the one human being who lives up to his part of the covenant. Whereas Israel lost faith in the wilderness, Jesus remains faithful and obedient. And because of that faithfulness he himself becomes the new and eternal covenant between us and God—a relationship that can never be broken, no matter how often we as individuals fail to be faithful.

In our election which we will celebrate Sunday we too shall be entering upon a special covenant with God. We are aligning ourselves with Jesus. We say that we wish to be baptized in his name—to join in the covenant which he created with God. We may fail to live like Jesus, we will sin and deny our true selves. But nevertheless God will be faithful to us. The covenant will never be broken or withdrawn. And God's faithfulness and love will draw us home to him.

In your prayer today read the appropriate story for this Sunday's liturgy. Use the story to shed light on your own experience of failure and sinfulness and of God's love, forgiveness and fidelity.

Move from contemplating God's outreach to us into your own response to God. In the story of Adam and Eve we see how the covenant was broken by them. Their infidelity brought sin and estrangement into our world. And indeed each of these covenants must contend with sinfulness. The covenant with Noah occurs only after God has punished humanity's sin. And, as we know, the covenant with Israel was again and again threatened by disobedience. It will be the same with us. We will fail to respond to God's love. And yet that love is still offered to us and God continues to make covenants with us until finally in Jesus an everlasting commitment is formed. So in your prayer today keep in mind your weakness, your own sinfulness. Yet in the midst of your betrayal keep in mind too God's constant striving to form a relationship with you and to draw you closer to him.

SATURDAY AFTER ASH WEDNESDAY

Cycle A — Romans 5:12 - 19
Cycle B — 1 Peter 3:18 - 22
Cycle C — Romans 10:8 - 13

These three epistles point out the breakthrough that has occurred in Jesus Christ—he is the basis for the new and everlasting covenant which God has made with us. Again and again in previous covenants the human side has failed to live up to the agreement because of sin and disobedience. But with Jesus all that has changed.

In the Cycle A reading Paul draws the parallel between Adam and Christ. Whereas Adam and Eve's disobedience brought sin and death upon us all so this one man's obedience has won grace, justice and eternal life for all people.

In Cycle B the reading from Peter points out that the flood was a prefiguration of baptism. Just as the flood washed the world clean and allowed us a new beginning ratified by the rainbow covenant, so our baptism will wash us clean and we will emerge shining with the resurrection of Christ.

In Cycle C whereas the first reading gave us Israel's confession of faith, Paul in the epistle tells how Jesus replaces Israel and so becomes our confession. Whereas Israel proved faithless to the covenant, Jesus' faithfulness makes him himself the new covenant. And in this new covenant all peoples are included. There are no longer any divisions; in Jesus we are all brought together to share the Lord's mercy.

We see then in each of these readings that no longer is there a need for us, through our own efforts, to maintain a covenant with God. Our own weaknesses and failings cannot destroy this new covenant, this new relationship of love and mercy which God wishes to shower upon us. We cannot and do not deserve God's love for anything we have done or can do. Instead God's love is a free gift to us. And that gift is Jesus Christ.

In your prayer today read carefully the appropriate epistle for tomorrow's liturgy. As the epistle speaks about Jesus Christ allow yourself in prayer to dwell on what Jesus has already given you. Recall what has already happened to you as a result of following Jesus. How has your life changed? Is there a feeling of peace, forgiveness, or love that was not there before? After you have spent a few moments in reflecting upon the gift of Christ and of baptism which he is calling you to, turn to your Father and thank him for reaching out to you and calling you to be a Christian.

MONDAY OF THE FIRST WEEK OF LENT

Bread, the key element in yesterday's ritual, is one of the most important symbols in Christianity. In the story of the temptation in Matthew and Luke, Satan suggests that Jesus feed his hunger by turning stones into bread. Bread in one form or another has always been a staple of the human diet. For many of the world's peoples it is the staff of life itself. Being such an important foodstuff it has a long history in the Judaeo-Christian tradition. Let us enter into some of that history.

Bread in our tradition is above all a symbol for freedom and liberation. When the Israelites were still slaves in Egypt and the plagues were falling upon the Egyptians, God told Moses that soon the people would be allowed to leave Egypt. But since their flight would be so hasty there was no time to leaven the bread for their journey. They would have to subsist on unleavened bread—bread made on the run. To this day the Jewish people celebrate the feast of Passover with that unleavened bread which recalls the flight from Egypt and their liberation so long ago.

Matthew's and Luke's accounts yesterday build upon the story of the manna in the desert. For after the children of Israel fled Egypt they wandered in the desert for forty years. While there, their faith was tested in many ways. Being hungry the Israelites complained and longed once more for Egypt even with its harsh slavery. But God sustained them in the desert with a miraculous bread that seemingly fell from heaven each night and could be gathered on the ground the next morning. In our story yesterday Jesus is presented as the new Israel. While the Israelites in the desert complained and called out for bread, Jesus does not do this. He knows that God will sustain him. He has faith. And he knows moreover that the word of God is more nourishing than even bread itself.

Bread played a part even in the far-off legendary beginnings of Israel. Abraham is the father of Israel and of Christians because of his faith and trust in God. When Abraham came to the land promised him by God, he met a rather mysterious figure: Melchisedech, the high priest of Salem. Melchisedech offers Abraham gifts of bread and wine. Here the bread is a sign of peace and an offering to the Lord in thanksgiving.

Bread plays an important role in the ministry of Jesus as well. Here in the desert he is tempted to turn stones to bread for food. But instead he relies upon God to sustain him. When he teaches his disciples how to pray, he tells them to ask for their daily bread— both the physical nourishment they need as well as the spiritual feeding which bread symbolizes.

There were at least two occasions when Jesus performed a miracle with bread (Mk 6:30 - 44; 8:1 - 10). Each time there was a large crowd of people gathered to hear him. The disciples grew worried because there was no food for such a crowd. But Jesus took their loaves and fish, blessed them and passed them to the crowd. Miraculously each person ate his or her fill.

In John 6 Jesus speaks of himself as the bread of life. He himself is the Word of God among us; he provides us with our nourishment for growth and well-being. Once more physical feeding and spiritual nourishment are linked by the symbol of bread.

What of our own Lenten experience? Are we becoming more aware of the spiritual dimension of our own life? All too often we can see our life only in terms of the physical—what we do, where we go, who we are. But our Lenten practice can awaken us to the larger dimensions of our life. Spend time in your prayer today reflecting upon how the spiritual side of your life has been nourished recently. How has our Father supplied you with the daily bread you need so that you might grow in the Lord Jesus?

TUESDAY OF THE FIRST WEEK OF LENT

So far we have been considering the story of Jesus in the desert in terms of the individual. How did Jesus encounter temptation and resist it? How do we in our Lenten practice come to see temptations for what they are? But there is another dimension to this story which we discover if we examine the original story upon which our present one is modeled. Mark simply presents a story of Jesus' temptation, but Matthew and Luke amplify Mark's account using the story of Israel's temptations in the desert as a model. Temptations do not merely happen to individuals like Jesus or ourselves; they grab hold of entire nations and peoples as well.

The first temptation concerns hunger and the bread that promises to satisfy it. Israel after she had escaped from Egypt wandered through the desert for forty years where she was tested. Unfortunately Israel was unequal to the test and failed consistently. First she grumbled about the lack of food. "We shall die out here in the wilderness," the people complained. "Why did you bring us out here only to starve us?" In response to the people's complaints God showered the miraculous manna on them from above.

In Jesus the Gospel writers see the embodiment of the new Israel who is totally faithful to God. Where the old Israel failed and sinned, Jesus is able to resist temptation. When he grows hungry he relies upon the Lord to sustain him. Here is a faith and trust in God lacking among the ancient Israelites.

Similarly we ourselves as individuals and nations are often so preoccupied about material things that we grumble and fight among one another. At such times we would, if we were truthful, regard faith as weakness or even resignation. Yet this story shows it is not so: for Jesus was sustained and so shall we all be if we but trust in God rather than our own devices. This trust does not excuse us from concern about material needs for ourselves and for the needy, but it can prevent us from making such needs the only ones requiring satisfaction.

The second temptation takes Jesus to the temple where he is told that if he is really God's Son he should demand some spectacular sign as confirmation. Again this is a temptation we all might relate to, both as individuals and as a nation. We are told we are loved by God but what proof do we have? As Israel wandered through the desert she also grew doubtful about God's love for her. Is this any way to treat a chosen people? "We want more proof of God's concern for us," the people demanded of Moses. So Moses took his staff and struck a rock. From the rock flowed forth water.

When asked to demand a sign for himself Jesus replies to Satan that you shall not put God to the test. In our own life we can take Jesus as our guide. Yes, we want assurances that we are on the right track, that we are growing in the Lord, that we are doing the right thing. And there will be times of assurance, such as Jesus experienced at his baptism. But the rest of the time we are counseled to take what comes. At times we may feel foolish following Jesus. We will believe ourselves naive to think that we were loved and chosen by God. Such feelings are quite normal. St. Teresa once complained that if this is the way God treats his friends no wonder he has so few. But Jesus is our model. He did not scream and shout that he wanted concrete proof here and now of God's favor. He simply continued doing what had to be done, satisfied that things were in God's hands.

Similarly in our own life as individuals and as a nation how often are we caught judging ourselves and others? Did I do the best I could? How are we better than others? We are the good guys and therefore the enemy must be the bad guys. And we even expect signs that this is so; wasn't our defeat in Vietnam so hard to accept because we always believe God to be on our side and we expect signs of this such as victory? We want to hold ourselves up as God's chosen people with all the privileges we believe should go to such a beloved.

How much better would it be to take example from Jesus? He does not exult himself, gathering titles, privileges and miracles to bolster his self-image. He simply lives his life day to day, confident in God's will for him. Jesus does not live as though he were the center of the universe; we do. That is our sin, our pride, and we might learn from his humility. We could learn this lesson both as individuals and as nations.

For the final temptation Satan takes Jesus up a high mountain and promises him all kinds of power if he will but worship him. For power is Satan's gift to give. Power achieves great things in this world. Power works for us. Israel recognized just this need for power. "It is not enough to have God on our side," she complained. "We need a king like the other peoples; we want to develop our political and economic clout. We want to take our rightful place among the nations." And God gave in to their demands and provided Israel with a king.

In our own lives we often crave power and use it as well both as individuals and as nations. As parents we may want to raise our children by the power of love alone, but how quickly we lose confidence in love's power, resorting instead to the power of force. Nor are we any different as a nation. How can we call ourselves, as some do, a Christian nation when we increase the arms race and stockpile weapons hoping that such a show of force will bring about the kind of peace we claim to desire?

Jesus too is tempted by power. Being the Messiah he should be able to wield power wisely. He will not let it go to his head. He wouldn't use power for his own selfish ends. Things could be different if Jesus seized power; the world could be set right.

But Jesus sees through the game. Any power which is force will not set things right. Jesus will rely only upon the power of God which, as St. Paul says, seems like weakness in the eyes of the world (1 Cor 1:18 - 25). So Jesus refuses to take Satan as his god and receive the gift of power. He remains loyal to the true God, knowing that only by doing so is there real hope for a better future.

We might use Jesus' example to examine our own life and that as a nation. How often do we resort to force and strength in the hope of bettering things? And why have all the forces throughout history not brought us out of misery but only created more and more conflict and evil? Down deep inside we do not trust in the power of love alone. But can we at least begin to trust in that power? Yes, it appears weak in the eyes of the world. But so did Jesus. What might happen if we began to act out of the power of love? How might things be different? We, like Jesus, might end up on a cross. But is that so bad considering what the outcome of the first crucifixion was? And how much can we really hope for from our traditional use of power?

Let us explore these temptations in our prayer today. Choose one that speaks to you and your own situation. Imagine the way you usually handle the temptation by giving in to the spirit of this world. What might it be like to approach the temptation as Jesus did? Also look at the way in which groups and nations have also fallen to this temptation. Pray for them in your prayer as well. Ask what you might do in your own small way to lead people out of such worldly ways and into the way of Jesus.

WEDNESDAY OF THE FIRST WEEK OF LENT— REVIEW

We began our Lenten journey just one week ago today. Each Wednesday we shall stop to take a look at our journey. Look back now over the past week. What were the highlights? Were there moments of prayer that were special for you? Did something happen that you would like to reflect upon more now? What were the difficulties? Has your attitude toward this Lenten journey changed during the past week? Perhaps you began with a burst of energy, but then as you entered the week that energy dissipated. Examine your resistance to your prayer journey. Was prayer easier at one point, more difficult at another? Were you faithful to your prayer or did it die away at some point? How do you feel right now as we begin our second week?

As you do this reflection try not to fall into judgment. If you missed your prayer, it will do no good to blame yourself or tell yourself that you have failed. Simply accept the reality and go on from there. Instead of judgment see whether you can discover why you were unable to pray. Did you choose too much for yourself? Was the time wrong? Did you think of prayer or your practice as a heavy burden that weighed you down? How might a change of attitude affect things? Have you tried considering your prayer as a happy and light time when you can be nourished by God? Or do you consider it only a duty that you or others have imposed upon you? It is much more important to discover something about ourselves than to blame ourselves. But we can only do this if we are not judgmental about our work.

If you are not content with your journey this week and would like to change something about it, ask God for help in this re-evaluation. Do you want out because you have undertaken too difficult a task or simply because you do not want to confront these parts of yourself? Remember, Lent is a time when we look at the deadness in ourselves, when we confront our ego that tries to rule us by power and fear. It is not easy to confront this deadness and this power. We might be tempted to respond with force and might or to give up altogether. If you are tempted to give up, ask yourself whether already you might have learned something about yourself, the world (Satan) and God. What more might you learn should you persevere? Of course you cannot do it alone. You are not meant to do it alone. We have one another in our community, and above all we have our Father. When we encounter this deadness or this forcefulness the way to deal with it is not to combat it but instead to surrender to God—he will sustain us and raise us up just as he raised Jesus. Keep a lightness about your Lent and it will be so much richer for you.

Chapter Six

THE SECOND SUNDAY OF LENT

The Readings: Cycle A — Genesis 12:1 - 4; 2 Timothy 1:8 - 10;
Matthew 17:1 - 9
Cycle B — Genesis 22:1 - 2, 9, 10 - 13, 15 - 18;
Romans, 8:31 - 34; Mark 9:2 - 10
Cycle C — Genesis 15:5 - 12, 17 - 18;
Philemon 3:17—4:1; Luke 9:28 - 36

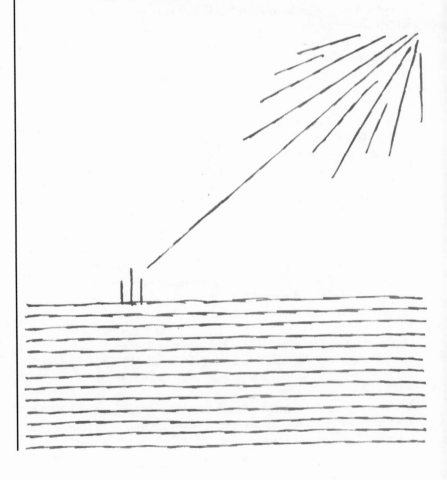

THURSDAY OF THE FIRST WEEK OF LENT

Cycle A — Genesis 12:1 - 4
Cycle B — Genesis 22:1 - 2, 9, 10 - 13, 15 - 18
Cycle C — Genesis 15:5 - 12, 17 - 18

Today we shall begin examining the lessons for next Sunday's celebration. Each year's lesson is a story about Abraham, our father in faith. And common to each lesson is the promise of blessings which will come to Abraham. Abraham was blessed because he had faith in God (Cycle C). He had faith to follow God's call to leave his home for a distant land (Cycle A). He had faith when he was told to take his only son and offer him as a sacrifice (Cycle B). And as a result of that faith Abraham was blessed.

How often when we hear God's call are we uprooted and taken to new places! We might prefer our life to be more predictable and settled. Perhaps that is even the reason we thought of becoming Christians. Yet as we see from the example of Abraham who is our father in faith, when the call of God breaks into our life things are seldom the same afterward.

But while we might fear the unknown involved in the faith journey, still it is just this pilgrimage that we long for. For our past life does not satisfy us entirely; otherwise why should we have desired to follow Jesus? There was something missing or even stale about our existence. We longed for more than we had. And that longing has brought us to the Christian community.

Our desire was answered by God's call to us. We celebrated that calling in our election last Sunday. And our call, like Abraham's so long ago, will change our life; it may even disrupt it.

Yet because we have dared embark on this journey toward faith we are promised blessings. By accepting God's invitation to follow him on pilgrimage toward his Kingdom we are assured that our life will be enriched. Blessings will be showered upon us. For our faith journey itself will enrich our life. Nothing can happen to us as long as we remain where we have always been comfortable. But as we join with our new-found Christian community, journeying together toward the Kingdom we can support one another, drawing hope and strength from our fathers and mothers in the faith such as Abraham and Sarah. Their example will sustain us. And as we grow to know one another better we will discover our life filled with blessings it did not know before.

For today's prayer take Abraham and Sarah as our own models. Imagine yourself in their shoes, called to leave behind all that is beloved and familiar, told to sacrifice your only child, promised a far-off blessing you will never see. Yes, it is hard. What would you find most difficult to abandon? What fears might you have about the future? All of these fears and difficulties are part of our dying to ourselves.

But as we are learning, whenever we die, the Lord raises us up. So let our prayer move on to the promise of blessings for Abraham and Sarah. Again enter into their situation. They will leave their homeland behind but they will also be the parents of a whole new people. Millions will look to them as models for faith. What blessings might lie ahead for us on our own pilgrimage? There may be all sorts of things we expect and want of our faith. But let us not become entangled in them now. Instead remain quietly in prayer with just the promise of blessings coming toward you. Allow God now, if he wishes, to provide a hint of the happiness that might come. Often we do not even know what we want or what will make us truly happy. Certainly at this point in the story Abraham does not know what concrete form the blessings will take. And in Cycle B the command to kill Isaac seems to negate what he has been promised. The blessings he imagines may be quite different from the blessings he will receive. It may be quite the same with us. So in our prayer let us simply dwell upon God's promise of blessings. Let us be thankful that we have been called to this journey. Let us take courage and find peace in God's promise that by embarking upon a faith journey our life will be blessed.

FRIDAY OF THE FIRST WEEK OF LENT
Cycle A — 2 Timothy 1:8b - 10
Cycle B — Romans 8:31 - 34
Cycle C — Philippians 3:17 - 4:1

Paul tells us that we are called not because of anything we ourselves have done but rather because of God's own purpose for us; we are saved by his grace (Cycle A). Today, reflecting upon this great theme of our redemption, we shall learn to pray in a way that opens us to God's grace.

If we are not aware that it is God who calls us and brings us to wholeness we can get into a lot of trouble. For example, we might wonder why we have been chosen. We do not feel that we are adequate to be entrusted with the good news of Jesus. We are limited human beings. We may not be able to do what is expected of us. After all just what did God see in us to choose us in the first place?

But as Paul explains, we are not chosen and called because of anything we have achieved on our own. We are not called because we have proven ourselves worthy or able; indeed we cannot do so for we are not worthy or able. We have been called simply because God has chosen to call us. And why does he call us? In a sense we can answer that he calls us because he loves us with a love that has been clearly shown in Jesus.

We see the extent of this love. For while God spared Abraham the distress of sacrificing his only son Isaac, he does not spare himself the anguish of seeing his Son Jesus handed over to be killed. He surrenders Jesus for our sake, that through him we might be made whole. And if God has done this much for us, we need fear nothing (Cycle B).

Knowing that we have been called we might also fall into the trap of wondering how we will accomplish what God wishes us to do. What if we fail? How can we succeed? Will we be adequate to our ministry? How are we going to be made whole and find salvation?

But as Paul tells us, our wholeness and salvation are not something we accomplish. Indeed we cannot achieve it at all. Our attempts are doomed to failure. We will be saved, made healthy and whole by God's grace through Jesus Christ. And that grace has already been granted us. It has sustained us in the past even when we did not recognize it, and it will continue to sustain and transform us in the future.

Nor is this wholeness which God offers us in Jesus something we can take for granted. Our transformation is not something that will take place only in the Kingdom. It must begin now. If we claim to follow Jesus, then our lives must manifest his vision, his way of life. If we have awakened to the vision of the Kingdom, then our hearts must not still be attached to the values of this world. If we are spiritual people, then our lives should not be overly attached to the material (Cycle C).

Then what is our task? Our work is to respond to God's call, to accept the grace given us. Faith is not won by us; it is given us by God. There is, however, something we can do. We can cooperate. We can learn to be still and listen to the call of God. And we can learn to respond to that call. By listening to the promptings of the Holy Spirit we will find our way home to our Father and his Kingdom. By learning to empty ourselves—by dying to ourselves as Jesus did—we make room so that we might be filled with the gifts of the Holy Spirit.

For your prayer today focus upon the Scripture passage appropriate to next Sunday. Read it over slowly. Let the words and ideas sink in. If a phrase or even a single word touches you or has power for you, remain with it; let it lead you deeper into prayer.

Let your prayer become a contemplation of Jesus Christ. He is our hope, our salvation. Allow Jesus to be present to you in your prayer. Let him show you the extent of God's love for you.

SATURDAY OF THE FIRST WEEK OF LENT
Cycle A — Matthew 17:1 - 9
Cycle B — Mark 9:2 - 10
Cycle C — Luke 9:28 - 36

The three Gospels for this Sunday tell the story of Jesus' transfiguration on the mountain. Here for a brief period Peter, James and John have the veils lifted from their eyes and minds so that they see the glory of God which dwells in Jesus. Now they see him as he is: the fulfillment of both the law represented by Moses and the prophets in the person of Elijah.

While the story describes what might originally have been a mystical experience for both Jesus and his disciples, Christians see the transfiguration as an image of baptism and of transformation. We can explore this image more deeply by taking first the experience of the disciples and then that of Jesus himself.

These three disciples have been with Jesus over a long of time now. They have heard his parables about the Kingdom. They have absorbed his teachings. They have seen the signs and miracles by which Jesus reveals the Kingdom to the people. In addition at numerous times in the Gospels Jesus calls these three apart from the others. Obviously they are special—they may understand his mission more than the others.

Now he takes them up the mountain with him to pray. And there he is transfigured before their eyes. Before, they had hopes and dreams that Jesus might be the Messiah. But now those hopes and dreams are being confirmed. Here is Jesus talking with both Moses and Elijah: the most holy figures of Israel's past. And they are showing him respect and homage.

Similarly in your baptism you will encounter Jesus in a new way through this sacrament. Like Peter, James and John you have been following Jesus for a long time. But like them a new dimension of your relationship with Jesus is about to occur. On the mountain the disciples have a foretaste of the resurrection. And in your baptism it is just Jesus' death and resurrection into which you will be plunged.

But the transfiguration concerns not simply the disciples' experience. What must it have been like for Jesus himself? The accounts tell us that his body is transformed, illuminated, his garments white as snow. And here are Moses and Elijah speaking to him.

And our baptism will not simply be an encounter with Jesus in the pool. In that pool we too shall be transformed, born again, raised into the light and life of Easter. We too shall hear the voice say about us that we are the beloved sons and daughters of God—children by adoption in Christ's baptism. A whole new life will open before us.

We cannot at this point anticipate what the experience of our baptism will be like. Indeed it is best to approach it with a sense of openness. But the Church has chosen this Gospel to help us prepare for baptism. Here is one way in which the experience of baptism might be put into words and images. And we can use this story in our prayer today to guide us toward our own baptism.

Read through the appropriate account for tomorrow's liturgy. Read slowly. Stop to savor what is happening. If a word or image strikes a chord with you, remain with it a while.

You might want to enter into the story by taking the part of one of the disciples. Imagine the long climb up the mountain. What might you be thinking and feeling? How do you experience Jesus' transfiguration? What does he look like? Allow the scene to suggest itself to your imagination.

At some point you may wish to move over into Jesus' experience. How does he experience this transfiguration? Imagine the radiance in your body—the light, the clarity, the peace.

To conclude your prayer speak to your Father about your own approaching baptism. Ask him for guidance as you prepare for this encounter with Jesus. Bring to him your fears as well as your hopes for transformation.

MONDAY OF THE SECOND WEEK OF LENT

The theme of "glory," which appeared in yesterday's Gospel, might introduce today's prayer. Unfortunately this word has lost much of its significance for us, but it forms one of the great themes of the Scriptures. For glory means more than a joy or a radiance. When the glory of God appears in the Bible it is a sign that God himself is present and revealed to us. Nor is God's presence merely for show; when God is present with his people he is liberating and saving them.

At the beginning of Israel's history the glory of God is first revealed. In Hebrew the word "glory" carries a sense of weight and power; it is also associated with clouds. As the Israelites leave the land of Egypt they are led by a cloud during the day and a pillar of fire by night. It is God's glory which guides the Israelites to safety. In the

Gospel story yesterday the cloud again symbolized God's presence now manifest in Jesus.

Throughout Israel's history the cloud of glory continues to be a theme for God's presence and blessing. Before Israel is conquered by Babylon Ezekiel foresees the destruction of the temple (10:18 - 22). He sees the cloud of glory leaving the temple site and interprets this to mean that God is abandoning his stubborn people to their enemies.

The cloud of glory appears at the beginning of the New Testament as well. When the angel Gabriel announces to Mary that she will mother the Savior he tells her that the Most High will overshadow her—again the image of the cloud as a sign of God's presence.

The image of the cloud as a symbol for God's glory has continued to be part of the Christian spiritual tradition. Last week in our prayer service we used a form of contemplative prayer. One of the most influential Christian books on this type of prayer is an eleventh century English classic *The Cloud of Unknowing.* The anonymous author describes contemplation as entering into the cloud which shrouds God. We penetrate deeper and deeper. And seemingly things grow darker as we journey into the cloud. But in spite of the outward darkness we are drawing closer to God. Indeed it is only through our increasing sense of unknowing that we can finally come to know the true God at all.

Today for our prayer let us take this theme of glory as our subject. Perhaps you may want to spend the time in contemplation as we did in the prayer service. You might use a candle or an image of Jesus to focus your gaze. Do not try too much. Simply be present to the meditation. When you find your mind wandering, gently return to the meditation.

For another kind of prayer you may choose to spend the time recollecting your own experiences of the glory of God. If it is a nice day you might take a walk. And on the walk keep yourself open to what you see, hear and feel. For ultimately the whole creation is God's glory and can lead us closer to him.

Finally you may want to pray with Psalm 23 that we used in the prayer service. Read through the psalm slowly. If phrases or words speak to you, pause and let them sink in. Perhaps the psalm will call you into silent contemplation of God's glory.

TUESDAY OF THE SECOND WEEK OF LENT

We have seen that the Gospel of the transfiguration is a foreshadowing of our own approaching baptism. And in our prayer this week we have explored and anticipated that baptism. But the experiences of transfiguration and of baptism are not ends in themselves. They are part of an overall context of life. Although Peter may want to build tents on the mountainside and stay there perhaps forever, the vision fades and Jesus takes his disciples down the mountain and back into the business of life.

For the disciples the transfiguration is another revelation of just who Jesus is. They had been with him, seeing the signs, hearing the parables, receiving instruction. They had come to know him well. Already they had inklings that perhaps Jesus was the Messiah for whom Israel awaited. Indeed, Peter, impulsive as always, had already confessed that Jesus was the Messiah. Now on the Mount of Transfiguration their hopes are in a sense confirmed. Here are Moses and Elijah deferring to Jesus. He must be the Messiah.

Before the transfiguration, when Peter had confessed Jesus as the Messiah, Jesus explained that he must go up to Jerusalem where he would be handed over to the authorities and killed. This did not fit with the traditional image of the Messiah. The Messiah was a glorious being, not someone destined for rejection and death. Peter sought to dissuade Jesus and was instead rebuked. The disciples may have discovered that Jesus is the Messiah, but just what kind of Messiah he is they have still to learn. There is still much to accomplish after the transfiguration.

And we might look at our own approaching baptism in the same way. Yes, we have spent much time studying the Gospels, learning about Jesus, experiencing Christianity. We may be tempted to look at our baptism as the climax of our pilgrimage, and in a real sense it is. But it is not the end of our journey—only a turning point.

Until now we have been discovering Jesus and his Kingdom. We have been receivers more than givers. Yet in becoming Christians we have decided to give public witness to our belief in Jesus. We are committing ourselves to live by certain values in our world. We are putting our lives in the service of the Lord. We are undertaking God's continuing mission in the world on behalf of the poor, the blind, the suffering. After our baptism our Christian lives will turn more and more in this direction of service.

In the Gospel stories of the transfiguration only St. Luke dares describe Jesus' experience of the event. What do Moses and Elijah tell Jesus on the mountain? They point out to him the way of his death. They point toward Jerusalem. For Jesus the transfiguration must have been the most glorious moment of his life. Here is a confirmation of his ministry to his disciples. Yet in the midst of the glory lurks the spectre of death. And Jesus in obedience accepts that death.

And what will be our own commissioning in our baptism? Through our acceptance of baptism we are proclaiming to the world our allegiance to Jesus. For most of us this may be an easy and joyful event. But some of us will feel pain as well. Our allegiance to Christ may separate us from our family or friends who do not understand our decision. And it is not too far-fetched to foresee a time when Christians again may face persecution and oppression. It is happening in many parts of the world today.

Christianity never offers us an easy joy divorced from pain. Such joy is ultimately deceitful and shallow. True joy must take account of pain and suffering and triumph over them. Baptism will not answer all the questions of our life. It will not make things easy. And it will be a long time before we are able to integrate this good news into our ordinary living. Like the disciples coming down from the Mount of Transfiguration, our journey is not over. There is much more to go.

In your prayer today join with your Father in looking forward a little. Are there difficulties or problems you see? Are there fears? Do you need help now in dealing with other people's ideas of Christianity? Bring these concerns to your Father. Ask for strength and wisdom. If there are fears, can you in prayer surrender them and trust in God?

WEDNESDAY OF THE SECOND WEEK OF LENT—REVIEW

Today completes another week of our Lenten prayer and practice, so we shall take the opportunity again to review our experience to this moment. First let us consider our prayer and practice this week. Were there times of difficulty? Were there days when you were unable to pray or to fulfill your contract? If so, how did you react? Did you let the failure depress you? Did you scold yourself for failing? Or did you treat it lightly by saying that it was not important anyway? Both these extremes do us little good.

When you have missed a day it is best simply to begin again. Do not reproach yourself on the one hand. And on the other, recognize that you have made a commitment and will continue to honor it.

Let us reflect back upon the prayer service last week. Were there any difficulties for you here? Were you able to enter into the prayer service? Are there aspects of contemplative prayer about which you have questions?

Moving on to our Sunday liturgy, recall that experience now. Could you enter into the prayer? Did the ritual illuminate any part of Lent for you? Were you able to enter into the ceremony with the oil? Do you begin to perceive the presence and meaning of symbols in your own life? Can you relate them to what we have learned of Jesus and his relation to these symbols?

Now let us consider our experience this last week. Ask whether it seemed a heavy load weighing upon you or whether it appeared light and fulfilling. Sometimes we are tempted to make our practice quite weighty. Yes, it is important to pray. And prayer is serious. But it need not be heavy. After all in prayer we allow God an opportunity to touch us. Such an experience cannot but make us lighter, happier, and more blessed. If you noticed heaviness creeping in, ask today whether you can find ways to lighten your prayer and practice in the future. Often it is sufficient simply to remind ourselves to keep it light.

Now let us look more closely at your Lenten practice. If you were not able to persevere this last week can you discover what prevents you from fulfilling your contract? Our practice is designed to reveal our ego. And the ego does not enjoy being exposed and uses all means available to defeat such attempts.

Perhaps you felt fear, or you missed one day and the sense of failure kept you from picking up and beginning again. These and many more are merely games of ego. Our Lenten practice is not meant to make us perfect. It is merely a means to help us see and know ourselves better in the light of Christ. If we can learn to spot the means by which ego maintains control over us we can also learn to be free of these games; this is our Lenten task.

All we need for this Lent is what we can handle this Lent. It is quite impossible to fix everything all at once. There will be plenty of Lents after this for us to tackle other problems. If we make the stakes too high we build in defeat and actually strengthen the ego's hold over us. If you have experienced difficulty in this area go back to the story of Jesus in the desert and enter into his experience again. Can you feel a little of his calm in handling Satan? He does not engage in hand to hand combat. Nor does he allow Satan to choose his weapons for him, which would mean fighting on the adversary's terms. Jesus simply refuses to engage in the ego's games; he will not be deflected from his mission. His example might serve us all well in our Lenten experience.

Chapter Seven

THE THIRD SUNDAY OF LENT

The Readings: Exodus 17:3 - 7; Romans 5:1 - 2, 5 - 8; John 4:5 - 42

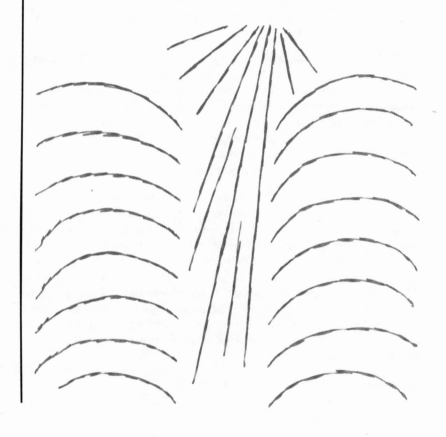

THURSDAY OF THE SECOND WEEK OF LENT
Exodus 17:3 - 7

Once more let us preview the readings at this Sunday's liturgy. The Old Testament reading hearkens back to that special time of Israel's birth. The slaves had escaped from Egypt and crossed over the Red Sea. Now they find themselves in the desert and begin to have thoughts about their situation. At least in Egypt they had the security that comes of being a slave. Were they brought here to this wasteland simply to die?

It should not prove too difficult for us to identify with the Israelites. Every one of us has embarked upon something new this Lent. We are filled with hope and enthusiasm that we might be able to persevere and truly be transformed. But once we are in the midst of the situation we realize just how unstable and uncertain it is. Who would have thought in Egypt that anything could be better than freedom or worse than slavery? But then there was no consideration of the hardship such freedom might bring.

Perhaps you can relate with the Israelites over your own decision to become a Christian. Yes, it seems very appealing to follow Jesus, and his promise of new life is certainly wonderful. But now that we draw near to baptism and are in the midst of Lent we begin to see the cost as well. Like the Israelites we find ourselves in a wasteland. We may be wondering whether we can persevere. We may begin to question whether we even should continue. After all was our old life really so bad? And is this new life as a Christian truly going to be worth the cost? And what in the world are we doing right now with this Lenten practice of putting obstacles in our own way? Is it all worthwhile?

Of course our questions and issues may be much more serious. We may be struggling through a particularly difficult period in terms of our relationships. We may have problems with our job. We may be plagued by illness. All sorts of concerns can place us in a position similar to that of the Israelites. Take time in your prayer today to discover what in your own life causes you to doubt, to lose hope, to complain bitterly. Let these things lead you into today's reading. In your prayer give voice to your concerns just as the Israelites did.

But just as the Israelites were not stuck and abandoned in their wanting and complaining, so let us discover whether our own prayer might not take us out of ours. Moses hears the complaint of his people and brings it to the Lord. God responds by telling Moses to take his staff and strike the rock. As he does so water pours forth for the people.

Although we do not have Moses with us today we might in our reflection be able to perceive a similar sign of God's care given to us. We have explored our life and found things with which we need help. Now let us ask Jesus to be with us. We do not have the strength to make it on our own. Left to our own devices we would die in the desert just as the Israelites would have.

But we are not left to our own devices. If Christianity says anything, it is that God does care for us and help us. The sign may not be anything as strange and wonderful as the water flowing from the rock, although it might well be. Never underestimate God's power. Once we have asked Jesus for help, let us continue our prayer by looking back over our problems and concerns with the aid of hope.

Hope has been debased in our culture even more than love. We tend to think of hope as weak—a last-ditch effort when all else has failed. But hope for a Christian is quite real and very important; it is one of the three great virtues along with faith and love. And hope at its most basic means the ability to imagine a good outcome.

So let us now enter into that virtue of hope and look for its seeds in our own situation. You have asked God to help you. Now relax (you can follow your breathing for a few minutes to help you). Once relaxed, consider your situation again. Can you imagine a possible future reality that might give you hope? Are there indications of hope that you simply did not see or take seriously before? These seeds might be concrete things or simply a feeling that matters will turn out all right. Allow that hope to grow and nourish you now just as the sight of water from the rock quickened the hopes of the Israelites.

FRIDAY OF THE SECOND WEEK OF LENT
Romans 5:1 -2 , 5 - 8

Our second reading next Sunday contains one of the most beautiful ideas of Christianity and one that can ease our Lenten journey. The thought is found in the last line of the epistle: Christ died for us when we were still sinners. Let us explore how we might understand this idea in our daily life.

Perhaps we are tempted to begin thinking that we are really accomplishing something through our Lenten practice. Maybe you have really been able to accomplish what you set out to do. Say, for example, that you decided to quit smoking. Now it is over two weeks and you haven't had a cigarette; this is wonderful. But for a Christian such success is not the whole of what we are about. Indeed for a person on the spiritual path success can be more dangerous than failure at times. If we had failed already we would be confronted by it and might have fallen into despair. Hopefully, however, we would pick ourselves up and begin again while asking God for strength.

But when we are successful we tend to become proud as well. See what I have done. I feel great. Perhaps there is nothing I cannot do.

Things are really going wonderfully for me now. Alcoholics Anonymous which is based on the spirituality of Jesus points out the dangers of such an attitude. Once the alcoholic stops drinking he or she is tempted to believe that he or she is cured of this malady. I have raised myself up from the bottom of the barrel. But from this attitude it is merely a small step toward believing you have the power to stop at one drink. Yet as Alcoholics Anonymous knows so well it is precisely that one drink that will cast the person back into the barrel. The alcoholic is never cured, and the only way that he or she can stay sober is through the help of God. You cannot do it on your own, for there are too many traps and pitfalls.

But alcoholics are really not so different from everyone else. We have not accomplished what we have done under our own power. As Paul states quite clearly, we have no power whatsoever to get ourselves out of the mess we are in. There is no way we can do anything. So when we manage to persevere with our practice or do anything else, before we begin to feel good about ourselves and what we have accomplished we might realize that we have been enabled by the grace of God which has been with us all along. Even when we were sinners Jesus died for us—he showers us with the grace, the ability, the power to be whole.

This attitude is not the same as the attitude of downgrading or self-criticism which is quite destructive. We are not purposely putting ourselves or our accomplishments down. We are simply keeping a proper perspective. Our ego would love to believe that it enabled us to do something. It will easily take the credit and so strengthen its control over us. We become inflated as Jung said, or proud as Christianity terms it. And St. Thomas Aquinas speaks for the Christian tradition when he names pride as the most deadly sin because in pride we place ourselves in the center of the universe and kick everything else including God into the background.

As Christians we accept ourselves as good and loved. But we also know that we are weak and liable to fail. We know that we can do nothing to help ourselves. However, even when we were totally astray, Jesus accepted death so that God's love for us might be revealed. And God will certainly help us now.

In today's prayer look at your practice or something else you have done. Reflect on the power of God that enabled you to accomplish the task. Then move on to reflect on the love of God Paul describes: this love for sinners, for those who are unworthy. How wonderful it is to be aware of this love that heals and saves us. How beautiful to be given this gift we did not earn. And we do not ever need to earn it, for there is nothing we can do to deserve it. In prayer give thanks for and rejoice in this love which has brought us so far and will carry us all the way home.

SATURDAY OF THE SECOND WEEK OF LENT
John 4:5 - 42

At tomorrow's liturgy we will celebrate the first scrutiny together. But this word "scrutiny" needs some explanation, for it does not mean that we are going to be questioned about the faith. Rather in its prayers the Church is asking that you become able to see your life more clearly in the light of the Gospel. And as we come to know ourselves in the light of Christ we see more clearly our sinful and selfish ways and how they have led us into darkness and unhappiness. As we prepare for baptism we can dare acknowledge our shortcomings and weaknesses, together with the sins and injuries we have visited upon others. Seeing ourselves so clearly we can then ask Jesus to heal us and bring us to the new life he has promised.

Our new life as Christians will begin with baptism when we are plunged into the waters of Jesus' death and raised into the glory of his resurrection. In tomorrow's Gospel one major theme is water.

Jesus speaks to the Samaritan woman about a water that will quench all her thirst. The woman wants such water and asks for it. We have done the same in our pilgrimage. We have heard the words of Jesus concerning his Kingdom. We have expressed our desire to follow him so that we might have a share in that Kingdom.

But it is not simply a matter of following Jesus or asking for water. Jesus answers the woman's request by revealing her misery: she has no real husband, and she has had five in the past. Such a history betokens a troubled spirit. The woman is obviously thirsty—not for ordinary water, but for the water of love, acceptance and care. She has not found such water in her attempts at wedlock. But in Jesus she sees once more that water she has always been seeking, the water that will satisfy her completely.

And what of us? With Jesus' help can we dare look into our own past and our present as well? How have we been seeking the water that quenches all thirst? How have we failed to find it or been disappointed? In your prayer today look into your own life. It is not easy to confront our faults, our failures, our sins. But not to be aware of our sinfulness keeps us stuck repeating the same mistakes. Like the Samaritan woman we may go through five husbands never realizing why we are unable to make a marriage or find the love we so desperately seek. But if we can confront our sins in the presence of Jesus we might be freed from them. The woman is not destroyed by what Jesus knows about her. For her it is a sign that he must be a prophet and can indeed provide her with the water. So we too have come to believe on our own journey.

In Lent we take a hard look at ourselves. We acknowledge the mistakes. We can be honest about our selfishness, our fear, our lack of trust. And this knowledge will not lead us to despair. All this can be our past; it need not be our present or our future. Tomorrow all will pray with us that we be freed of our thirsts and our misguided attempts to slake them. As we approach the waters of baptism at Easter we may leave them behind as we are plunged into the water that quenches all longings. Today recognize these thirsts and the mistakes you have made in your attempts to assuage them.

MONDAY OF THE THIRD WEEK OF LENT

The symbol of water has extremely important connotations in Christianity as well as in yesterday's Gospel. Today and tomorrow in our prayer we shall enter more deeply into this symbol so that it can speak to us concerning our own journey toward baptism.

Today we will explore the universal meanings of water. To do this first begin by taking a few minutes to center yourself. Assume your prayer posture, close your eyes and place your attention upon your breath for a couple minutes. As thoughts enter your consciousness, allow them to leave again while you return your attention to your breathing.

For our meditation today we will focus upon the element of water. Keep your attention upon the idea of water and allow associations of water to arise in your consciousness. Try not to censor. There is no need to find explanations for what arises; simply accept whatever comes up and hold it in consciousness for a moment. Then return again to the primal image of water and wait for another association to arise. Continue this for the duration of your prayer today.

The text below is merely to help you should you hit upon dry spaces in your meditation. You may not need it at all. These phrases are meant to spur your imagination, not to substitute for it.

A cup of water to quench thirst . . .
A bath to remove soil and dirt . . .

The coolness of water on a summer's day . . .
Clouds as a promise of rain . . .
Rain itself refreshing the earth and making things grow . . .
Floods and the threat of waters overwhelming us . . .
Ice and snow . . .
The beauty and stillness of a new snowfall . . .
The treachery of ice . . .
The crystalline purity of ice . . .
The soothing and calming of a warm bath . . .
Hot tubs . . .
A glass of ice water . . .
The thrill of swimming . . .
Water skiing . . .
Skiing in the snow . . .
The fun of a water fight . . .
The terror of drowning . . .
The horror of dying of thirst . . .
The threat of a flood . . .
The rivers of red water that course through our veins . . .
One of the four primal elements . . .
The majesty of the sea . . .
The trickle of a brook on a summer's day . . .
The calm beauty of a lake . . .
The majesty of the thunderstorm . . .

TUESDAY OF THE THIRD WEEK OF LENT

Today we will continue our meditation upon water, but we shall
move from the natural associations of water which occupied us
yesterday into the meanings which water has taken on in the Judaeo-
Christian tradition. After you have read through this material, allow

the images of these various stories to remain with you. They may reveal deeper meanings as you meditate upon them. Then if you like you may look up the original stories in the Bible and read them over prayerfully.

Water goes back to the creation itself in our tradition. Genesis 1:1— 2:4 tells how in the beginning God breathed upon the waters and brought forth all of creation. Here the water symbolizes chaos itself, for water unless it is contained in a vessel is quite formless and flows wherever there is least resistance. As we picture the beginnings of creation through the eyes of this Hebrew poet we can see those formless waters like the vast waters of the sea. Then the breath of God moves over them and the myriad creatures come forth. Here the water becomes a sign of fertility and suggests the waters of the womb or the primeval stew from which life emerged.

Another ancient story, Genesis 6:5 — 8:22, tells of the great flood in the time of Noah. Noah was a holy man whom God chose to save from the general carnage and ruin. Noah was told to build an ark and take two of every living creature into it. Then the rains and the floods came, destroying everything on earth. It rained for forty days and nights—the time of our Lent—but Noah and his family and all the creatures on board were safe. Finally the rain ended and Noah wondered whether it would be safe to leave the ark. He first sent forth a raven, and then a dove twice. The second time the dove returned bearing an olive branch—a sign of peace ever since. Then Noah and all the creatures left the ark. God placed a rainbow in the sky and by it promised Noah and his descendants that never again would he destroy the earth. In this story we see how water wiped out sin and allowed for a new beginning for creation.

The escape across the Red Sea is the most famous story involving water in the Old Testament. Pharaoh finally allowed the Israelites to leave Egypt. But as they fled he changed his mind and set off in pursuit. All seems lost as the Israelites come to the shores of the sea. What will happen now? But Moses stretches out his staff and the waters divide. The Israelites pass through on dry ground. But when the chariots of the Egyptians try to follow them through the sea bed they become mired in the mud. Soon the waters return and the army is destroyed. Once again we see the waters associated with both life and death, liberation and destruction. The water brings freedom to the Israelites but is destructive of those powers that would crush liberty in our world (Exodus 14:1–31).

Water plays an important part in Jesus' life and teaching. We have heard how he promised the water of eternal life to the Samaritan woman. At the very beginning of his ministry he was baptized by John in the river Jordan. Then the heavens opened and Jesus knew that he was God's Son and beloved of God. This knowledge commissioned him to preach the good news of God's Kingdom. Here water is associated with God's acceptance and favor; we might link it as well with the waters of birth. God declares Jesus his Son in the baptism almost as though he had given him spiritual birth from the Jordan waters (Matthew 3:13 - 17).

At the end of Jesus' ministry water is once more present. When Jesus was dead on the cross a Roman soldier pierces his side with a lance. St. John says that both blood and water flow from this wound. As Christians we believe that Jesus saves us and makes us whole by dying for our sake on the cross. This water flowing from his side is an image of baptism by which we enter into Jesus' death and are raised with him to new life (John 19:31–37).

Indeed water encircles our entire tradition. We have seen it at the beginning of creation. In another creation story we see how Adam was placed in a garden where the four great rivers of antiquity had their source (Genesis 2:5 - 14). And at the very end of the Bible, St. John, looking forward to the consummation of this world, describes the new heavenly Jerusalem coming down from God. Once again the rivers of living water are present for our nourishment (Revelation 21:1–21). Truly water is one of the most important symbols and can reveal to us much of the good news we have received from Jesus.

WEDNESDAY OF THE THIRD WEEK OF LENT—
REVIEW

As we have each week let us take time today to review our
pilgrimage into the third week of Lent. To begin your prayer return
in your mind over the past week as you have done before. Have
there been difficulties? Crises? Have any insights arisen in your
prayer or elsewhere? Perhaps instead of going back over the details
of the week you would prefer to simply sit and ask for an image of
this week's journey to present itself to you. When an image arises
allow it to unfold for you. There is no need to analyze it in order to
understand its meaning. Let the image give rise to its own
associations.

One of the great obstacles to the spiritual path is the temptation to
use the same means here we might use in solving some other
problem or dilemma. We search the evidence to make sense of what
has happened. But prayer and spirituality will not yield to willful
effort; trying harder will not work here. In prayer we are hoping to
contact the deep wells of our being. Imagine a well similar to Jacob's
well in last Sunday's Gospel. These wells are not open to our
ordinary rational powers. God gifts us with eternal water through
dreams and perhaps fantasies. We might be tempted to believe that
our prayer has accomplished nothing if we judge it as we might
judge our progress in mathematics. But it cannot be evaluated in the
same way. So in our review this week let go of some of these
rational means or worldly ways of evaluating our journey.

Instead let us remember that even in this review we are primarily
praying. Begin with your centering prayer. Then ask yourself about
this last week: How have we drawn closer to Jesus? Are there ways
we came to see the truth of Jesus: that in every death there is the
possibility of resurrection? Did we come closer to tasting that water

that quenches all thirst? We might answer "yes" to these questions and yet not be able to provide any specific instances in proof. That is all right. In the quiet and calm of our prayer God may draw us into the deeper significance of our week.

Also let us beware of the worldly habit of judgment that might come into play. We are not putting ourselves to the test here to discover whether we made progress or not. There is no means of failing in our examination today. All we are doing is discerning our path this last week. There is no good path versus a bad path; there is only our path which hopefully has been touched by God. In our prayer let us ask God to show us some of the ways we might have been touched and even healed.

Chapter Eight

THE FOURTH SUNDAY OF LENT

The Readings: 1 Samuel 16:1, 6 - 7, 10 - 13;
Ephesians 5:8 - 14; John 9:1 - 41

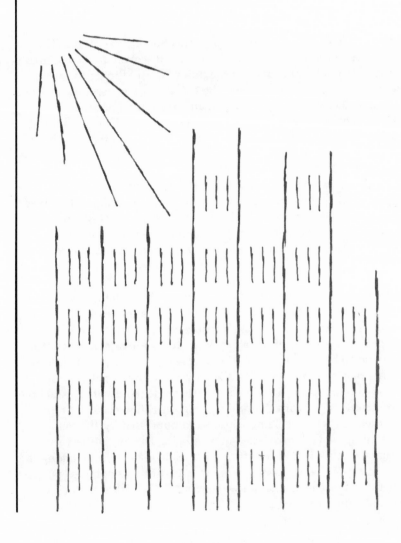

THURSDAY OF THE THIRD WEEK OF LENT
1 Samuel 16:1b, 6 - 7, 10 - 13a

Today we shall again look forward to this Sunday's readings. The Old Testament lesson tells how David was discovered and anointed to be the king of Israel. Samuel the judge was told to go to Jesse's family. Immediately Samuel sees the eldest son and assumes that this is the one chosen as king. Yet again and again the Lord rejects the obvious choices. Finally the choice comes down to David who is still a young boy and a shepherd. Yet this unlikely lad is the one chosen by God.

We might pray with this story as a reflection upon our own being chosen. Other people might be more qualified to become Christians, yet in the mystery of God's call we have been selected. With whatever gifts or failings we have, upon us the choice of the Lord has rested; he has chosen us to carry his good news today in our world. This choice will always remain a mystery.

Yet there is no mistaking the fact that throughout the Old and New Testaments God's choice is revealed not only as the least obvious in human eyes but as the weakest possible choice. David is the youngest and least fit of Jesse's children to be king. Jesse himself has no reason to be seen as a father of kings—he has no power in Israel. For that matter Israel herself is always a rather weak nation when compared to Egypt or Babylonia on either side. And within Israel the Lord identifies not with the priests, kings or ruling class but rather with the poor who are being abused and oppressed by the rich. Finally in Jesus God becomes a human being lacking in the very powers we think would benefit a great leader—he is from among the poor, he has no power of his own, he is part of an oppressed people. Sometimes it seems as though weakness itself qualifies us for God's love and support.

As we consider our own situation we come to see that we were not chosen because of any great ability. The mystery is one of love: God chose us because he loves us, just as he chose David simply because he loved him. And the Old Testament is full of songs of love for this shepherd chosen to be king.

We can see further that the people dearest to this loving God—his people in the world today—are those who are poor, weak and lacking in power. Among the suffering is our God to be found. He suffers with the poor and lives with the hope that such suffering might cease. As we look forward to becoming Christians we join in solidarity with God's people—the poor and outcast of this world.

For prayer today put on Samuel's experience in this story. We are told to go out and anoint God's chosen king. Where would we look in our world? Like Samuel we might be tempted to go to the great, the talented and the mighty. And indeed many of these people might identify themselves as chosen by God. Yet the Scriptures tell us that such is not the case. God's love and concern, the place of his presence in our world, is not in the comfortable corridors of power but rather among the hungry, the lowly, the overlooked, those who wait, the so-called useless members of society. These are the people to whom God's heart goes out. These are the people Jesus ministers to. In becoming Christian we too are taking upon ourselves God's love for the poor. In today's prayer let us make the poor the center of our concern. Let us ask how we who perhaps are not really poor or powerless can help alleviate the suffering of others. In our reflection let us seek to see in the lives of the poor and suffering the holiness, the promise, the royalty which Samuel came to recognize in the shepherd boy.

If our Christianity is only for ourselves, then it is selfish and the vision neither of Jesus nor of the Hebrew Scriptures. As we become Christians we become people who live for the sake of others. Can we bring these neglected others into our consciousness today and every day in our prayer? Can we through our prayer ask how we might like Samuel come to recognize God's compassion for these people and act to alleviate their suffering? Today we pray to be enlightened so that we might know where God is present in our world. We pray also that we might be able to feed and serve him there. For as often as we do this to one of the least of our brothers and sisters we do it to Jesus.

FRIDAY OF THE THIRD WEEK OF LENT
Ephesians 5:8-14

In this Sunday's epistle Paul speaks of two different ways—that of light and that of darkness. Let us explore these different ways while continuing our theme from yesterday of God's concern for the poor. Our attention today will not be upon our individual morality but rather upon how we are part of a people who are of light or darkness.

Throughout the Scriptures and especially in these words of the prophets the consistent theme is that oppression is wrong, that to be involved in riches and power at the expense of others is sinful. These are among the deeds of darkness of which Paul speaks. All too often Christians have reduced their vision to a purely private morality. "I have to keep my nose clean, and that is all that is expected of me." But such a vision goes directly against the Gospel. We are responsible for our brothers and sisters, for Jesus laid down his life for his brothers and sisters.

Let today's prayer begin to make concrete for us just what the paths of light and darkness are. What are the ways by which we allow injustice to flourish in our world, our nation, our community, our family? Let us look at ourselves and how we contribute to these structures of oppression. And we do contribute to them if only by our indifference to the way things are. Yes, there is not much we as individuals can do to alleviate hunger in the world. But we are not simply individuals—at the very least we are part of a Christian community. And there are things we can do—if not to solve the problem, at least to take steps to make things slightly better.

Let us consider our own works of darkness. Are we indifferent to the plight of others? Do we lie to ourselves and tell ourselves that the poor are lazy and deserve what they have? Do we fail ever to see ourselves in the place of those more unfortunate than we? Are we so wrapped up in our own problems that we do not see how much worse off most of the human race is? Do we support structures and government policies which favor the rich at the expense of the poor? Such policies have been around since the time of the prophets and are still here today. In America some have said that we favor capitalism for the poor and socialism for the rich. How concerned are we to extend ourselves to the poor with our money, talents or time?

Now following Paul's advice we will try to discover what the Lord wants of us. It is certainly more than keeping our noses clean; it is more than an individual morality. Jesus defined his mission in terms of the outcasts in his society. As Christians we shall be taking that ministry upon ourselves. How can we extend God's love to those whom no one wants—those in nursing homes, those in prison, those in mental institutions, those on the bread line?

We might consider our own lifestyle as Americans. Do we really need all the goods we have? Might we not get along with less, particularly when the less might enable a sizable portion of the world's peoples to move out of starvation? Might we learn ways to be less wasteful of the world's goods? Christians cannot afford to shrug their shoulders, claiming that such ideas are simply not economically or politically feasible. The voice of God has been quite clear for over three thousand years, and that voice identifies itself with the poor and their condition. In becoming Christians how are we going to take real action to stop the exploitation and oppression which are a part of the world? Of course we have no hope of winning on our own. We can no more solve hunger than we can save our own soul. But we can cooperate with God in each instance. If we put our lives in the service of God—not necessarily in extraordinary ways but simply in ways that we find ourselves called to through prayer and our Christian community—who knows what strides might be made toward that day when the Kingdom of God will dawn and every tear will be wiped away?

SATURDAY OF THE THIRD WEEK OF LENT
John 9:1 - 41

Tomorrow at the liturgy we shall celebrate the second scrutiny together. Today let our prayer prepare us for that celebration. Yes, we have already examined ourselves last week. We might be tempted to believe that any second or indeed third scrutiny will only cover the same ground. But it need not be so. Each week we can look at our life from another perspective, in the light of another symbol. We might also consider different areas of our life and faith each week.

Since this week's prayer is concerned with the implications of being a Christian in terms of social justice and help toward others, let us take this as our theme today. In tomorrow's Gospel we shall encounter the man born blind who was healed by Jesus. Once more we meet the theme of darkness and light which we found yesterday in Paul's epistle. Here is a man blind from birth who, through the touch of Jesus, is able to see. Putting ourselves into his predicament we might come to view our own faith journey differently. Most of us are not physically blind. But we are nevertheless blind in many ways. In our encounter with Jesus many of the blind spots have been exposed and perhaps even healed. Today in our prayer let us look closely at our areas of blindness so that we can ask to be healed like the man in the Gospel.

We begin our prayer by centering ourselves. Observe your breathing for a couple of moments. Once more remember that as we look at ourselves it is not with judgment and condemnation or with pride and congratulation. We admit our blindness so that we might be healed and made whole. When you are sufficiently relaxed and recollected, look back over your life to areas where you are blind. Pay particular attention to blindness in areas of social justice and charity. Were there times when you did not believe you had any responsibility toward those less fortunate? Were there times when the poor simply did not form part of your concerns and world? What other areas of blindness have been revealed to you as you came to know Jesus and his vision? Are there areas in which your blindness has been healed? Are there still places where you are in need of healing? Are there areas where you are only beginning to recognize your blindness?

Take time now to explore your life using this image of blindness. Do not search frantically. Allow the memories to arise on their own within your consciousness. Try not to censor them. They may be painful or embarrassing, but that is all right. We are bringing them up not to chastise ourselves or hurt ourselves but so that the Lord might heal them for us.

When you have considered your areas of blindness let us move in our prayer toward asking Jesus to lift that blindness as he did with the man born blind. Some areas may be healed already. Others are in the process of being healed. Others may still need real healing. Simply present them one by one to Jesus.

Our blindness may not be healed right away, if ever. But in our prayer let us imagine what each healing would be like. Take one of the blindnesses that is particularly hindering you now. As you present it to Jesus allow your imagination and hope to picture what its healing might be like. Again do not use too much effort. Remain relaxed but receptive. Allow pictures to present themselves to you. We may think that we know just what it should be like to be healed of this blindness, but let us put such strong ideas aside. Instead allow the Holy Spirit to suggest ways in which we might be healed. These may not necessarily be the way we think it should be or even the way in which it will happen. But if we are receptive to them we are on the road toward real healing.

MONDAY OF THE FOURTH WEEK OF LENT

Our prayer and meditation concerning justice and charity this last week may have raised problems and questions. When we awaken to the injustice and oppression in our world there is a good chance we can be overwhelmed by the enormity of the situation. How can we possibly commit ourselves and begin such a huge task? Isn't it presumptuous to believe we might do any good at all? And how can we sustain and nourish ourselves so that we do not burn out? How will we cope with failure?

Such issues are quite real and threatening, but there is a Christian response toward them which we will explore today. When we awaken to the needs of our neighbor we enter upon a life of charity and justice-making. As in every endeavor there are temptations involved. It is easy to begin seeing ourselves as the saviors of the world. We see our side as good and the other as the evil enemy. Once the battlefield is defined our own work becomes crucial if not central to the struggle. And it *is* crucial; the mistake is in seeing it as our work or struggle. It is first and foremost God's struggle. When we place our life in the service of justice we are really cooperating with God in his work. And if so we must struggle God's way. We must guard against our own self-righteousness. God works through love and compassion; if our tools and strategies are different are we not in some way betraying the Kingdom?

We are learning that true meditation is not something we do. Real meditation teaches us to let go of our control so that the Holy Spirit may guide us. The same issue is involved in our work in the world. If we see it as our work, accomplished by our effort, fueled by our sense of justice, we are fated either to fail, to burn out, or to be co-opted by the forces we are attempting to replace. How many revolutions succeed only in supplanting one tyrant with another?

In the desert Jesus refused to play the game according to Satan's rules. When Satan offers him power Jesus does not accept, although we might believe he could have turned it to his own ends. But to accept such power would keep Satan in control of the world; things would be no different, perhaps even worse. Instead Jesus looks to the will of his Father rather than his own will. He cooperates with the will of God which does not work from power but love.

Jesus' prayer is often just this surrender to the will of his Father. He teaches his disciples to pray, "Thy Kingdom come; thy will be done." When we operate out of our own will, then only our own kingdom will come, leaving the world the same as ever.

On the night before he dies Jesus again prays to his Father. He is frightened. He probably does not know whether his mission has been a success or a failure. From the vantage point of that Holy Thursday night it must have appeared a failure—soon he would be betrayed by his own disciple, abandoned by the rest and condemned by his own people. There is nothing he would not have done to escape such a situation. Yet he ultimately prays that his Father's will be done—perhaps the most difficult prayer on earth.

Can we make that prayer our own as well: Thy will be done? In our prayer today let us seek to know God's will for us. Let us commit ourselves to following that will in our life. We have heard the pleas of Jesus and the prophets for the poor and hungry. We have awakened to our neighbor and know that we must find Jesus there. We do not know where this will lead us, but are we willing to be guided? Are we willing to surrender our own will which has brought us very little happiness if all were known? Are we willing to place our hands into God's hands so that we may be commissioned, sent forth and supported on the way? It will take the rest of our life to discover God's will and to surrender to it. All the way to our death we may feel we are walking in blindness—but so did Jesus that night in the garden. Yet as the great poet Dante discovered, only in God's will lies our peace.

TUESDAY OF THE FOURTH WEEK OF LENT

Today let us bring together all of last Sunday's readings. We began with Samuel anointing David to be king of Israel. We have seen how this anointing represents God's choice of David to be king. So have we all been chosen and so shall we all, like David, be anointed. By his anointing David is the king that God has chosen for Israel. God's spirit comes to rest with him; through the Spirit's guidance he will become a great king.

And why should we need such an anointing? Why do we need the Spirit of the Lord? We discovered in the second lesson that there are two ways—of light and darkness. Left to our own we tend to choose the way of darkness. We are so far from being whole that often we cannot even see which is the better way for us. But when we allow the Spirit to direct us, when we ask direction from the Lord and seek to make his will our own, then we will be led into the ways of the Spirit.

We could say that being anointed by the Spirit is much like being cured of our blindness. The Spirit reveals the truth to us. Now we can see clearly what before may have been dark and obscure. Surely already there have been instances in our faith journey when suddenly we understood in a deep way what before we had been blind to.

But our anointing in the Spirit makes us more than simply a people cured of blindness. David was anointed to be the leader of Israel. Jesus was anointed with the Holy Spirit as the Christ. "Christ" means "the anointed one." When we are anointed we are made into Christ. In putting on Christ we put on his ministry, his mission, his Spirit. We may have come to Jesus seeking a better life for ourselves. But our life is transformed in Jesus when we cease living for ourselves and begin to live for others. As Christians we find our wholeness when we give our lives in service on behalf of God's Kingdom.

We are becoming members of the Christian community. Jesus is present among us still. Within our community his ministry continues—the blind see, the lame walk, the captives are freed and the poor hear the good news. Let us enter into that ministry with our imagination. Are there things in our community—people, causes, issues—which need the healing of Jesus? How might you and other Christians be messengers of the good news in such situations?

Begin by asking the Spirit to open your eyes so that you may see with the eyes of Jesus. Become aware of projects that are already happening in the church community. These missions could use your help and talents. Then consider what might hinder you from entering into these activities. Finally ask the Holy Spirit to be with you and to use all God's people as instruments of peace. It is certainly true that we cannot do everything that cries out to be done. But is there some ministry of help where you feel a call to involvement? Take that ministry into your prayer: ask for guidance and strength to be responsive to God's call.

WEDNESDAY OF THE FOURTH WEEK OF LENT— REVIEW

Once more today we shall look back over the last week of prayer and Lenten practice. First, was there a real difference this week? Did some things become easier or more delightful? Did others become difficult? Did you experience resistance to anything this week? Can you see why there was resistance? Again, do not judge yourself; simply observe. Remain detached so that with distance and calm you may perceive things that were not so clear when you were in their midst.

Can you begin to see a pattern emerging from your Lenten experience? Do you feel yourself being led to certain experiences or understandings? What image comes to your mind now when you relax and ask yourself to see your journey so far? Allow the image to come to mind; try not to censor it. When an image arises, allow it to expand. Observe it for a moment or two. Allow any associations to arise. Keep a light touch—don't press too hard toward understanding. Consider many possibilities and rule out none.

Let us consider our attitude toward our Lenten work as well. Has that changed since the beginning? Perhaps you began with great enthusiasm which has now dried up. Can you see any reasons why such a change has occurred? Our best attitude lies somewhere between taking things too lightly and too seriously. Have we made our prayer heavier and more serious than it need be? Ask the Holy Spirit to guide you in this evaluation now and to lead you to a rewarding prayer attitude.

Let us look ahead in our journey as well. Are there any fears or concerns about what lies ahead? As Easter approaches have you experienced a real strengthening of your commitment, or are you not as sure anymore? It is quite all right to have such feelings. Negative feelings do not necessarily mean that you are not cut out for baptism. They are telling you something though. Spend some time with prayer, explore them alone now and later with others if you wish. You may come to understand what they mean.

Chapter Nine

THE FIFTH SUNDAY OF LENT

The Readings: Ezekiel 37:12 - 14; Romans 8:8 - 11;
John 11:1 - 45

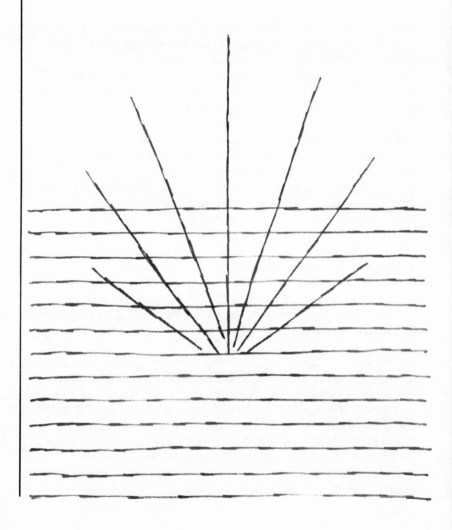

THURSDAY OF THE FOURTH WEEK OF LENT
Ezekiel 37:12-14

With next Sunday's readings we come upon the major theme of our journey—death and resurrection. Today we shall pray with that theme as it appears in the first reading from Ezekiel. As Christians looking back upon Ezekiel's prophecy we might read it as a description of the final day when the world will end and all will be resurrected—and certainly it can be so read.

But sometimes in Christianity our belief in the resurrection has been of a far-off event that will occur only after death or after the end of the world. This concentration upon the endtime blinds us to the resurrections occurring all the time in our very midst. And actually the words of Ezekiel do not refer to some far-off day but rather to now: "I am now going to open your graves."

During our journey this Lent we have again and again looked closely at our lives. We have allowed parts of ourselves to die, and we have seen that even in this dying there are already signs of resurrection. Our journey has taught us in a concrete and practical way the Christian hope that from every death God can raise us to new life; this is one way of speaking of God's action in our world.

Our reading of Ezekiel can also bring another neglected theme of resurrection to our attention. The emphasis upon the individual in our Western culture has made us forget that we are part of a family or a people. Yet it is just this national character that Ezekiel stresses. He is not talking about individuals rising from their graves; the whole people shall be brought alive again. Let us take that image of the resurrection of a people into our prayer.

We are part of a people now as we prepare for baptism and

reception. We, the elect, have come to know one another as we have prayed together on our journey toward baptism. On that night we shall all be raised again. Yet there is still much death and decay among us now. So let us in the beginning of our prayer today look at ourselves as this people preparing for baptism. Apply Ezekiel's promise to your community. Bring before the Lord the deadness that exists within you not only as individuals but as a people. Ask the Lord to open your graves and lead you back to the soil of Israel, the soil of the Kingdom.

Ezekiel's hope is not simply for a spiritual resurrection at the end of time. He is speaking concretely to the Israelites in their exile from their homeland. The resurrection that Ezekiel looks forward to is not a general resurrection of the dead but rather a freeing of Israel from exile and a return to the native soil. Here we come upon the political dimensions of resurrection.

In our world today many peoples are threatened with death and destruction because their liberty has been taken away by political or economic means. Our hope as Christians for resurrection includes a political resurrection for our sisters and brothers as well. In your prayer for resurrection bring to mind those people caught in the death of exile, poverty, discrimination, injustice, and war. For them we pray for an immediate resurrection so that they too might come to enjoy the bounty of our Father's creation.

Finally let us pray for the people to whom we shall soon be joined: the Church. As we journey through this world we are filled with signs of death and decay. But the Church while seeing the death still hopes for resurrection and new life. We hope for a resurrection that will heal the many wounds among Christians so that the body of Christ may once more be united. We hope for a resurrection from our worldly concerns so that we may cling only to the new life with which God graces us. We hope for a resurrection in our own particular Christian community so that we may awaken to our mission to bring Christ into the world and to transform this world so that all people may come to share in the resurrection Jesus offers to all people. Finally we pray for ourselves as we enter this Christian community, that we in our newness and our enthusiasm may be signs of the resurrection to those who have lost hope or become bogged down in the death that surrounds us.

FRIDAY OF THE FOURTH WEEK OF LENT
Romans 8:8 - 11

As we move from the first reading for next Sunday to the epistle we shift our exploration of resurrection from society to the individual. Just how can we experience resurrection? During Lent our practice has opened our eyes to much that is dead in us. Perhaps even our body through its weakness, sickness or old age is speaking to us of death. Certainly death is the surest thing about our existence if we allow ourselves to contemplate it. In the face of so much dying how can we possibly be resurrected? Can we be sure we are not simply whistling in the dark, hoping perhaps even beyond hope for something like resurrection?

There is a spiritual dimension as well. Now the spiritual might seem to be quite airy and unsubstantial but it is not really so. The spiritual side is not concerned with ghosts, spirits or fantastic miracles or even with the geography of heaven and hell. The spiritual is concerned with a vision of the world, with values for living and acting in the world, with concerns for the people and the ideas that concerned Jesus. Being spiritual simply means recognizing that what can be seen or measured is only a part of reality. Being spiritual means trusting in God to resurrect us rather than attempting to pull ourselves out of the grave by our own bootstraps. Being spiritual means following Jesus by casting out fear and worry, having compassion for ourselves and others, extending ourselves to those in need, trusting in love rather than might and power, and finding happiness in the Kingdom of God rather than in money or power.

As Paul suggests, when we turn our attention to the spiritual we find that we are brought alive by the Spirit of Christ that dwells within us. When we contact our spiritual side we are contacting the Christ within us. And when that contact has been made the door is open toward resurrection. Let us leave behind our old concerns and come alive to the spiritual.

In our prayer today let us turn toward the Spirit. Ask the Holy Spirit to lead you from material and unspiritual concerns toward the compassionate vision we have received from Jesus. Let your prayer be in quiet for a while so that you may hear and feel the promptings of the Spirit toward life and resurrection. Again we do this simply by following our breath as we did in the prayer service on the transfiguration.

You might wish to consider some of the death you have discovered in yourself. If so, simply bring it to the Lord. Do not condemn yourself for it. Do not make excuses for it. Simply bring it to mind and present it. Once you have done so again quiet yourself, remaining silent and open. Perhaps in prayer the Spirit may show you how even these dead bones can be resurrected. Conclude your prayer by asking for this resurrection for yourself, for the others elected to the sacraments, for the Christian community, for all the people of the world.

SATURDAY OF THE FOURTH WEEK OF LENT

John 11:1 - 45

At tomorrow's liturgy we shall celebrate the final scrutiny. Our Lent is now drawing to its climax. Today in prayer we will work with paper and pen to explore our Lenten journey. In all the scrutinies the Church prays that we may be separated from the things of this world and united to the vision of God's Kingdom. Each week we have prayed with different images and themes. First with the woman at the well we acknowledged our thirst and asked for water that gives eternal life. The next week we joined with the man born blind in asking for sight in our own darkness. Tomorrow we shall join with Lazarus who was raised from the dead. So let us now pass over into Lazarus' experience.

Take a sheet of paper and draw a line down the middle of the page. On the left side at the top write "death" and on the right side "resurrection." Now center yourself in prayer, asking the Spirit for guidance. All through Lent we have been consciously dying to ourselves so that we might be raised up in Christ. As you review your Lent jot down on the left side all the deaths you have undergone or become aware of. These may include truths you were blind to, attitudes which lead to death, sinful actions against others, fears, worries, sickness, depression, whatever form of death comes to mind.

When you have completed your inventory, then take some time to be with this death. Allow yourself to mourn as did Lazarus' sisters. This is a part of you that is dying or that is already dead.

Now let us pass over into resurrection. First of all go over your list again. Even now in the midst of death some of these deaths have passed over into resurrection. Perhaps if you experienced death as fear there were times this Lent when you were able to let go of fear; in those times you experienced something like resurrection. Are there already other signs of resurrection among your deaths? Describe them briefly on your paper in the right hand column across from the deaths they were raised from.

Of course there are bound to be other instances where resurrection has not yet made itself manifest. Perhaps this is a death that is not yet complete. Maybe you are only now dying here. But in your prayer can you ask to go through this death? Can you at least ask to be separated from this death so that resurrection may be open to you? You might be unable to imagine a resurrection. You are so close to what is dying that you cannot envision yourself surviving without this part of you. This is all right. True resurrection is always much more than we could imagine. But even if we cannot imagine what it will be like, we can remain in hope. Ask your Father to bring you forth like Lazarus into new life even though you have no idea what that new existence might be like.

MONDAY OF THE FIFTH WEEK OF LENT

Today we shall focus our prayer upon the theme of resurrection, so prominent in yesterday's liturgy. While the concept of the resurrection of the dead arose rather late in Israel's history it had a related idea which was at the heart of Israel's faith and which will allow us to see resurrection in a fullness that spreads far beyond the issue of personal death and immortality.

The idea of resurrection comes to be linked with that of liberation. The earliest Christians understood Jesus' death and resurrection in the light of the earlier story of Israel's birth and deliverance from bondage in Egypt. Thus when Israel crossed over the Red Sea she passed from slavery into freedom. Later Jesus accomplishes a similar passover; however this time it is from the slavery of death into the full life of his resurrection. As Christians we do not leave behind the experience of Israel as a way of understanding Jesus. Instead we examine our world for the existence of slavery today in the hope that through our life and service God may bring freedom to birth there as well. Thus the work God began with Israel and brought to fulfillment in Jesus continues in our midst today.

After you have centered yourself in prayer ask yourself the ways in which people are bound and in slavery today. Consider such things as economic slavery, the prison of addiction, psychological bondage, and political oppression. Then seek for signs even in these death-like situations where resurrection might break through. Are these situations only open to death or is there even here hope of new life?

Of course the primary impact of resurrection is upon physical death which hangs over all of us and often prevents us from living to the fullest. To explore this idea in our meditation enter into Lazarus' experience in yesterday's Gospel. Picture yourself lying in the tomb. Think of all that is now dead and done with—your life is over. The good and the bad is now all over and finished. Be neither too positive nor too negative about death—it simply is. There is no fear, no joy, no hope, nothing. There are things we are sad to part with, but there must be other things in our life we might be glad to let go of. Perhaps we can see from this vantage point in Lazarus' tomb just how much of our life was already dead anyway. Let those realizations come to you now.

Now as you lie in the tomb hear the voice of Jesus sounding even through the rock. He is calling you back to life. What does it feel like to be called by him? Everything you were is dead. You are dead. But now you are being given life again. What do you want and hope from this life that is rising in you? How will you enjoy it? What might you do with it? How will you consider it differently from the life you enjoyed before?

You have a new lease on life now. You have an opportunity for a new beginning. There is no need to take on anything now that was dead. You can leave all the death in the tomb. All you need to think about now is what you wish to be a part of your living today. Feel the life coursing through you. Feel the exhilaration. Feel the freedom. Feel the chance for a totally new being, a fresh start. To conclude your prayer take your concerns for resurrection to your Father and ask him to draw you out of death and into the new life which he has promised you in Jesus.

TUESDAY OF THE FIFTH WEEK OF LENT

In our prayer service this week we receive the Lord's prayer: the most sacred prayer for Christians. But this prayer is more than simply another set of words. Rather it is a guideline for all of our prayer. Today let us focus our prayer upon prayer itself.

We begin by examining our own prayer journey. What is the history of your prayer life? When did you first learn how to pray? Was there a time when you did not pray? Who first taught you how to pray? Have there been other teachers along the way? How has your prayer changed over the course of your life? Take some time now to recollect your experience with prayer. We include here not simply petitionary prayer but all kinds, from meditation to bodily prayer to petitionary prayer.

Now turn to your present prayer life. What are your concerns today? What forms of prayer do you use? How often do you pray? How important is your prayer to you? How satisfied are you with your prayer? Are there some things about prayer you find difficult? Do you have difficulty praying altogether? Are there other ways of praying you would like to explore?

Prayer does not exist for itself alone or even for ourselves alone so we should examine how our prayer affects our daily living. Does prayer help you to live more fully? Does your prayer enable you to be more loving and caring of others? Does prayer nourish you? Does it help you recognize and remove or overcome obstacles in your life? Does prayer turn your concerns toward others? Does it awaken you to the need for social justice in our world? Does it keep before you the needs of others? Does it enable you to minister to others in the spirit of Jesus?

Now let us consider the content of our prayer. Just what do you pray about? Make a list of things you take to the Lord in prayer. What are your reasons for praying? What do you hope to receive from your prayer? Are there things you do not bring to God in prayer? Are there things you consider inappropriate to prayer?

Finally let us dream a little about prayer in our future. What would you like your prayer life to be like? Are there kinds of prayer you feel called to in the near future? Are there kinds of prayer you would like to explore and learn? What would you like your prayer to do for you? Can you see any concrete things you can do in the near future to realize these dreams concerning your prayer life?

Keep in mind as you explore your prayer life that you are not here to judge or condemn yourself. Treat yourself with the same love and mercy with which your Father treats you. We are looking at our prayer life simply to gain a better understanding of what is happening to us. It does little good to blame ourselves for praying too little or poorly. Such an approach only makes us feel bad and guilty. But we can examine our prayer life to ask whether we would like to be praying more, or differently, or more effectively. Perhaps we feel that we are doing adequately right now. All of these are legitimate responses. Conclude your prayer today by taking your concerns to your Father and asking for what you need.

WEDNESDAY OF THE FIFTH WEEK OF LENT—REVIEW

Once more we will take inventory of our week and of our Lenten pilgrimage. We are now nearly at the end of our journey. So today we will look back over the entire journey. From right now what have been the real peaks and valleys of your pilgrimage? What have you learned? Where have you grown? What has remained just about the same? And how has the actual journey been different from what you originally anticipated?

Hopefully our Lenten journey has been one of self-discovery. Our Lenten practice has put a pebble in our shoe so that we might be a little more awake to our life and able to see our habitual thoughts and actions more clearly. What have you learned about yourself this Lent? How have you come to see yourself in a different light? What have you discovered about yourself? How have you changed?

Also consider your own consciousness. Have you noticed a change of awareness within yourself? Does your awareness seem to be greater than when you began? Have social concerns and the plight of the poor become closer to you this Lent? Do you sense a solidarity with the poor through your own fasting and practice?

Often Christians employ Lent to free themselves from practices and habits we have ceased to regard as useful to us. Has this happened to you? If your practice involved giving up something you were dependent upon, how do you view yourself in this regard now? What do you hope might happen after Lent in this area?

We undertake a Lenten practice to place conflict in our life. Hopefully this conflict will prod us to rely more upon God than we usually do. What has been your Lenten experience? Do you feel more reliant upon God? Do you sense that you have given up some control? Are you able more often to let go and allow things to happen rather than to be in control all the time? Is it easier now to let go in a situation?

As we approach the end of Lent we have probably uncovered many dead things in our life. Can you name some of those things you would like to let die and let go of? Also, what are the things you hope for from God to replace those dead and dying parts of yourself?

In doing this exploration let us not be too critical or expect too much. After all this is only one Lent, and our first one at that. We cannot expect major life changes (although they may be there). What we are really looking for are signs of change. Lent occurs in the early springtime when spring is more a promise than a reality. It may be the same with our life. We cannot at this point know all that our Lenten observance has accomplished. But we can look for those new green shoots that herald the spring, and we can hope. And of course we can take our concerns to our Father in prayer to ask for further guidance and assistance through this next week as well as in our future as his children: brothers and sisters in Christ.

Chapter Ten

PREPARING FOR HOLY WEEK

The Readings: Isaiah 50:4 - 7; Philippians 2:6 - 11
Cycle A — Matthew 21:1 - 11
Cycle B — Mark 11:1 - 10
Cycle C — Luke 19:28 - 40

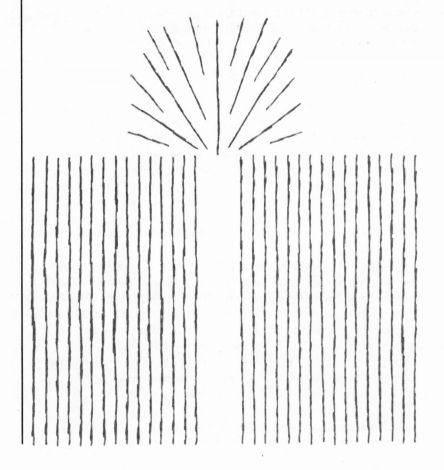

THURSDAY OF THE FIFTH WEEK OF LENT
Isaiah 50:4 - 7

As we approach next week we arrive at the climax of our Lenten pilgrimage. Now the themes of our liturgies become much more ominous. Jesus is moving toward confrontation with the powers of this world. And we also are headed toward our own encounter with his death and resurrection in the Easter sacraments. So in the next couple of days we shall move out of Lent and into the paschal fast to ready ourselves for this encounter.

Today we shall concentrate upon Sunday's reading. This passage from Isaiah speaks of the suffering servant upon whom Jesus modeled his own life and ministry. Let us, like Jesus, put on the experience of this servant. There will be times in our life when we shall be confronted by rejection, failure and suffering. These are not pleasant experiences, and usually we do everything possible to avoid facing such situations. But they are also an unavoidable part of living and dying. If we would find the wholeness which Jesus promises us we must learn to embrace all of life—the painful and the joyful.

As we pray over the first section we can identify with being chosen by the Lord. We too have been called by Jesus to follow him. We have become his disciples and have heard the word of God. We have also begun to minister in our community. Perhaps we have visited the sick, helped to feed the hungry, worked to improve our community. Allow Isaiah's opening words to recall to us our discipleship and ministry. Let us remember the joys we have had learning and serving. We might also remember the help and assistance we have been given to grow in the Lord.

Next Isaiah describes the downfall of the servant. His ministry is rejected; he is misunderstood. The love he brings is perceived as hatred, and hatred is the reward for his ministry. In our own life and following of Jesus we may find the same rejection and misunderstanding. You may have felt it already simply because you are becoming a Catholic Christian. Many people have prejudices about Christianity and Catholicism. It is difficult for them to understand what this means to you. Ponder these words of Isaiah— words which Jesus took into his heart as he wrestled with the rejection of his ministry.

If you have not experienced hardships so far you can still draw inspiration from this passage for the future. There is no promise that by becoming a Christian things will be easy. Our God will not remove us from pain and injury. Our religion will not be an anesthetic against all hurt. Indeed it may plunge us deeper than ever before into the pain of the world. Allow Isaiah's words to open that world of pain for you; we are now moving toward the cross and death.

But our walk through pain and rejection is not a walk alone. As the conclusion of our reading makes clear, God is with us even through the rejection, the pain and the dying. He comes to our help. He walks by our side. And we know also that Jesus has been here before us. In this next week Christians shall once again celebrate his death and resurrection. Because of his victory we can all take heart. Let the final words of Isaiah sink into your heart now. Perhaps you might read them slowly over and over again. Look back on the hard times in your life. From your present vantage point can you see that God was there with you all along? Many of the saints have said that those times when they have felt most alone and abandoned have truly been the times when God was closest to them. Has such been your experience?

Conclude your prayer by asking for God's continued support and presence as you walk through life. Ask him to show you the path through pain and suffering so that you may remain untouched by insults, unbroken by rejection. Ask that as we journey with Jesus through this next week we too might find the way to be faithful servants like the servant in this reading.

FRIDAY OF THE FIFTH WEEK OF LENT
Philippians 2:6 - 11

This Sunday's second reading is an early Christian hymn quoted by Paul in his Letter to the Philippians. In this hymn Jesus is shown emptying himself of all that is divine in him by right so that he may become a human being, even a slave, and subject to death. As we meditate upon this great hymn let us begin by putting ourselves into the situation of emptying. Have there been times recently, perhaps in your Lenten journey, when you have felt called upon to empty yourself? Have you been able to do so or did you cling to your position, your pride, what you felt by right was yours? What was the situation like? If you were able to let go and be emptied, what was that like? Were there any fears or other feelings associated with it?

Now use your own situation to enable you to enter into the experience of Jesus. He emptied himself of all that was divine so that he could participate in, share, and eventually redeem our human experience. Contemplate this great emptying. Feel the love that motivated God to do this for us. In our prayer today we are not trying to discover something so much as simply to be with and appreciate the great event of our salvation.

Now we move on to the exaltation of Jesus. We see that his path was through death, but it does not end there. And throughout the liturgies of next week we will see that the Church does not isolate Jesus' death from his resurrection—they are one continuous movement, one event. Jesus passes through death and is raised up, given the highest place, and made Lord over all creation. In your reflection try to grasp the sweep of this raising up; catch the exultation, the joy, the exuberance, the wonder, the power.

Now turn again to your own experience. In those times when you have let go and allowed yourself to be emptied, have you experienced this raising up? Can we believe what Jesus reveals to us—that emptying does not lead to destruction but that through dying we are raised to new life? Has our experience touched upon the same mystery? Can we see Jesus as a trailblazer who shows us the way to this exaltation?

At the hymn's conclusion we see Jesus enthroned over all creation. Through his emptying of himself, all of us and indeed all creation are brought home to our Father. Such an idea leads us to wonder and praise. So let us join in this hymn of praise to Jesus now in our prayer.

We can give thanks that Jesus has shown us the way through death into new life. We give thanks for the love that prompted God to reach out and bring us home to our true happiness. We give thanks that God has shared our human condition; he personally knows what we go through and suffer. We need never be alone, for there is one who understands and has been in our place. Ask that as we journey through Jesus' last days on earth we too may gain understanding for the place of suffering in our own life. We can ask that our own pain be redeemed and made meaningful. We can finally give thanks that Jesus has indeed saved us. It is not up to us to forge a path from death to life; it has been accomplished for us and is given to us freely. For this we join with all creation as we declare our love for Jesus as our Lord and Savior.

SATURDAY OF THE FIFTH WEEK OF LENT
Cycle A — Matthew 21:1 - 11
Cycle B — Mark 11:1 - 10
Cycle C — Luke 19:28 - 40

Tomorrow we move out of Lent and into Holy Week where we shall celebrate the event of our redemption. Our journey is drawing to its climax. The ceremonies of Holy Week are the most sacred and ancient of our tradition. The early Church kept the paschal fast during this week so that it might celebrate Easter with renewed mind and body. This great fast has disappeared as an obligation, but in preparation for Easter you might consider some fast as a way of participating in the passion of Christ. You might fast the entire week beginning on Monday and ending with the Easter Vigil. Or if a shorter fast seems preferable you might fast from after services on Holy Thursday through the Easter Vigil. The Church fasts and abstains from meat on Good Friday. Refer to the directions on fasting given earlier if you are not certain what this entails (see chapter three).

Now is also the time to consider setting apart time this next week for prayer and meditation. If possible plan to attend the sacred liturgies all through the week, especially those of the triduum: Holy Thursday, Good Friday, and, naturally, the Vigil. But can you set aside other time as well to pray and read the Scriptures? If at all possible set aside next Saturday for yourself and God. Get away someplace quiet where you can be alone. Maybe at some time you might pray with your sponsor or the other people preparing for initiation. The events we celebrate this week comprise the center of our faith. They are not just historical events which are over and done with. The death and resurrection of Jesus gives meaning to our lives today as Christians. We will be plunged into this event in our baptism. But for the event to touch us deeply and transform us we need to cooperate—to open ourselves to the Lord, to be receptive to the new life he gives us. We have the assurance of the Church that

Christ will be present at the Vigil. The question is whether we shall be truly present there. Our prayer and fasting can help ensure that second presence.

For our prayer today we shall consider the story of Jesus' triumphal entry into Jerusalem which we shall celebrate at the Eucharist tomorrow. In a way this story captures the full meaning of this week. In Holy Week we do not simply recreate the events of Jesus' last days on earth. We do not move from the Last Supper on Thursday to his death on Friday to his resurrection Sunday morning. Instead in each liturgy we celebrate the one movement of the pasch—from death to resurrection. Each liturgy emphasizes different facets of this event but the one movement is not broken apart.

And in the story of Jesus' entry into Jerusalem we can see the different elements of the week. First there is the joy and celebration. In a sense Jesus is coming into his Kingdom and being acclaimed as a king. But he is a different king. He comes humbly riding on an ass. Here is a king who will give his life for his people. And underneath the festive mood there is tragedy. Jesus knows that quite soon these very people will deny and denounce him. He has no illusions; he is traveling toward his death.

In your prayer allow the story to guide you. Experience the many strands of feeling here—the joy as well as the terror and sorrow. Remember that Jesus is going to his death so that we may have life. Bring the feelings this calls up within you to him now in prayer.

Perhaps you yourself have been close to death. Maybe you have experienced a reversal from triumph to tragedy such as Jesus did. Let these experiences take you more deeply into the story.

In concluding ask that you will be able to enter deeply into the spirit of Holy Week. Ask God to keep your mind on the Passover of Christ. Ask to realize more deeply God's great love for us to take on death and blaze a path through to new life.

Chapter Eleven

HOLY WEEK

Passion (Palm) Sunday

The Readings: Cycle A — Isaiah 50:4 - 7; Philippians 2:6 - 11;
Matthew 26:14 - 27:66

Cycle B — Isaiah 50:4 - 7 Philippians 2:6 - 11;
Mark 14:1 - 15:47

Cycle C — Isaiah 50:4 - 7; Philippians 2:6 - 11;
Luke 22:14 - 23: 56

HOLY THURSDAY

The Readings: Isaiah 61:1 - 3, 6, 8 - 9; Revelation 1:5 - 8;
Luke 4:16 - 21

GOOD FRIDAY - THE PASSION OF OUR LORD

The Readings: Isaiah 52:13 - 53:12; Hebrews 4:14 - 16; 5:7 - 9;
John 18:1 - 19:42

HOLY SATURDAY

The Readings: Exodus 14:15 - 15:1; Romans 6:3 - 11;
Matthew 28:1 - 10

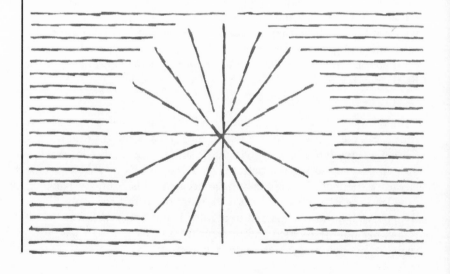

MONDAY OF HOLY WEEK

If we reflect upon yesterday's liturgy we may find it jarring that the triumphal procession of palms is combined with the tragedy of the passion reading—the account of Jesus' trial and death. And we move from the passion into the celebration of the Eucharist. Why this celebration in the midst of tragedy? Isn't there a place for each? Why together?

But that is exactly what the Church celebrates during Holy Week: the triumph in the tragedy. We celebrate this week Jesus' dying *and* rising: the passover, the pasch. Not three feasts, but one—the pasch. Jesus' passion, death and resurrection are one action: our redemption. It is that action we celebrate this week. And we do not retrace the steps as they were that first Holy Week. No, we see the entire action in each of the steps—the dying and rising in each part as well as the whole. So when Christians commemorate Jesus' passion and death we do it not to relive that event but to enter into it so that we may celebrate and give thanks for our redemption in it. Even while gazing on the cross on Good Friday we are mindful of the good news of the Easter dawn.

Jesus not only shows us that dying and rising go together; he does it for us. He dies for us, and we rise in him. This is the rhythm of Christian life: dying to ourselves and rising in the Lord. Look back now in prayer and see the patterns of dying and rising that you have already experienced. Some may have occurred this Lent. Go back now into the dying. When you were there did it not feel only like dying? And yet how it passed over into rising! This week we remember how Jesus died and rose for us, and we come to see the rising in his dying, and our share in his rising.

And if there is one thing we might learn this Lent, it is how long the journey toward wholeness is. Our Lenten practice may have produced significant change in our life, yet how far are we still from the total compassion of Jesus? Our Lenten practice may simply have pointed out our laziness, our weakness, our sin. How are we ever going to get anywhere, to become like Christ? Or perhaps our halting commitment and practice only cloaked our mediocrity. Is there room for the mediocre and ungifted in the Kingdom?

But this week we celebrate that Jesus has broken through to the Kingdom, and everyone who is joined to him is guaranteed entrance through him. So we can drop not our effort but our anxiety. In a sense the race is already over; we have won. We cannot make ourselves whole, but Jesus already has.

What needs saving, raising up, making whole in your life now? Bring it into this week. Let it die in Jesus so that it may be raised in him. For this is not simply a promise of eternal life in some far-off future. Eternal life is now. The resurrection is here even in our dying.

TUESDAY OF HOLY WEEK
John 18 and 19

Today we shall use the passion narrative of St. John as our prayer. And let us read it as Christians and with the Church: as an account not simply of Jesus' death, but of the good news of our salvation through Jesus' resurrection. In other words, although we shall be reading about Jesus' suffering and death we shall also be reading with John and the Church the good news of Jesus' resurrection and glory even here. For this is not history, the facts. Gospel is the meaning behind the facts.

For example, in the original trial of Jesus the situation is fairly standard. There is the defendant, Jesus, and his accusers as well as his judge, Pilate. And at the trial itself the weight was certainly on the side of the state. Yet when we read the Gospel's account of the trial we find a very different situation. Here Jesus is still on trial in an earthly court. But, as the Gospel makes clear, what is really on trial here is the entire system of worldly power and justice: Pilate and the Jews now become the defendants while Jesus is judge. But this irony was only made evident by Easter. Only at Easter is Jesus revealed in the fullness of his glory. But after Easter it is impossible for Christians to see Jesus except in the light of Easter. And that Easter light supplies the ironies for John's account of the trial.

Notice as well how the theme of renewed meaning through Jesus appears again. Pilate questions Jesus about his Kingdom. Pilate's ideas of a king are worldly, however. He does not understand this new kind of king. Like the woman at the well or Nicodemus he stumbles upon worldly understanding as Jesus tries to open him to a larger conception of kingship. Finally in exasperation he cries, "Truth! What is truth?"

And we too have stumbling blocks and misunderstandings of Jesus. We too become stuck in limited and worldly understandings. How does this Gospel account open our eyes to the light and expand our horizons of Jesus and life itself?

Finally we might call attention to John's description of the crucifixion. He speaks of blood and water flowing from Jesus' side when he is pierced by the soldier's lance. Now while this may describe the event, more than that is involved. John tells us that Jesus' mother is at the cross. The only other time she has appeared significantly in John's Gospel is in the story where Jesus changed water into wine: his first sign at the beginning of his ministry. Now she is present again, and again water is present. But instead of wine there is blood. For Christians wine is an image of Christ's blood in the Eucharist. These images link the death of Jesus to the Eucharist, to Easter, to the Church (of which Mary is an image). As you read John's account of the passion be open to these images and symbols. Through them John points to the meaning behind the events, the truth hidden in the facts, Easter's presence in the midst of Good Friday.

Spend your prayer time with this passion story. You need not read the entire account. If a particular passage has significance for you dwell with it. If your reading inspires you to speak directly to God, do so. How can Christians say grim events are good news?

WEDNESDAY OF HOLY WEEK

We have been looking at Holy Week so far in terms of the passover of Jesus. And we have discovered that the Church regards the passion, death and resurrection of Jesus as the one event of our redemption. But Jesus' passover also has historical roots in Israel. Jesus understands himself and his ministry in the context of Israel. And the earliest Christians, who did not have a New Testament of Scripture, found the entire good news of Jesus hidden within the Hebrew Scriptures.

Thus when Christians pray the psalms of Israel they do so not as Hebrews, but rather as Christians. Just as the light of Easter transforms the story of Jesus' death in the Gospels, so the light of Easter transforms the entire heritage of Israel for Christians. When Christians read the psalms they do so not as the original pray-ers would do. Rather they pray them in the light of Christ. And when we hear the great story of Israel's passover out of slavery in Egypt, we cannot help but connect it with Jesus' passover out of sin and death. Jesus does not replace these events of Scripture. He fulfills them. He makes them complete and whole. He perfects them.

Can we hope to understand Jesus outside the context of his Hebrew tradition? Jesus' Passover is not simply the story of his death and resurrection. It is also a retelling, a renewal of those other passovers: the escape from slavery and the birth of freedom. So when Christians celebrate the events of this week we not only remember Jesus' passover but also the passover of Israel. And when we remember Israel, we see there so long ago the seeds that come to fruition in Jesus.

For our prayer today we shall begin to use psalms, and we shall continue to focus our prayer upon these great songs for the rest of the week. Today our psalm gives thanks for all the great wonders God has worked for Israel. But as Christians we bring an added dimension to these prayers. We do not deny anything of the original, but we cannot help but see the presence of Christ moving in these great events.

First the psalmist praises God as the Creator. Many of the images call to mind the creation story in Genesis. And for us too God is the Creator who continues to bring forth life and light out of chaos and death. And, as Christians, we believe that we are created not only in the image of God but specifically through Christ. We are made in his image. Thus we see in the creation not only the original act of creation at the beginning of time, but also the re-creation that occurs constantly as we are drawn into Christ.

As the psalmist moves into an account of Israel's Passover allow the images to expand. We hear of God smiting the first-born of Egypt. Yet we realize that in Jesus he did not spare even his only Son for our sake. We give thanks for safe passage through the Red Sea, and we pray as well for our own passage through the sea of death in our baptism. We pray in remembrance of how he sustained the people with food in the desert. And we pray as well for the food that will sustain us at the banquet of the Lord which we will share at Easter.

And if Jesus brings Israel to fulfillment he also purifies her. There are passages in this psalm and in the Scriptures as well which seem quite brutal. God overthrows kings and peoples. There is much of the warrior in this God. But in the light of Jesus these images are tempered. We can accept them as part of our tradition. There is no need to be ashamed of them. Over the centuries the human race has indeed grown closer to God. What once seemed quite just now appears to us as savage. And what seems acceptable and even glorious to us may appear to our descendants as equally brutal and barbarous. What will future generations think about our wars, cold wars and arms races if they have grown to the extent of abolishing war as less than human? These psalms with their now archaic barbarity can keep us aware of our own limitations. And we can bring these limitations to God asking to grow more aware of his love, compassion and mercy which we have seen so prominently in Jesus.

Pray now with this psalm. Allow its images to refresh your memory of that first passover. And allow it as well to help you give thanks for and celebrate Jesus' passover. Stay with the psalm. If an image speaks powerfully to you, let it fill your prayer. If you quarrel with the ideas or images allow them to generate your own images and prayer. But let us give thanks to our God for freedom, for life, for his steadfast love.

Psalm 136

Alleluia!
O give thanks to the Lord for he is good,
for his love endures for ever.
Give thanks to the God of gods,
for his love endures for ever.
Give thanks to the Lord of lords,
for his love endures for ever;

who alone has wrought marvelous works,
for his love endures for ever;
whose wisdom it was made the skies,

for his love endures for ever;
who fixed the earth firmly on the seas,
for his love endures for ever.

It was he who made the great lights,
for his love endures for ever,
the sun to rule in the day,
for his love endures for ever,
the moon and stars in the night,
for his love endures for ever.

The first-born of the Egyptians he smote,
for his love endures for ever.
He brought Israel out from their midst,
for his love endures for ever;
arm outstretched, with power in his hand,
for his love endures for ever.

He divided the Red Sea in two,
for his love endures for ever;
he made Israel pass through the midst,
for his love endures for ever;
he flung Pharaoh and his force in the sea,
for his love endures for ever.

Through the desert his people he led,
for his love endures for ever.
Nations in their greatness he struck,
for his love endures for ever.
Kings in their splendor he slew,
for his love endures for ever.

Sihon, king of the Amorites,
for his love endures for ever;
and Og, the king of Bashan,
for his love endures for ever.

He let Israel inherit their land,
for his love endures for ever.
On his servant their land he bestowed,
for his love endures for ever.
He remembered us in our distress,
for his love endures for ever.

And he snatched us away from our foes,
for his love endures for ever.
He gives food to all living things,
for his love endures for ever.
To the God of heaven give thanks,
for his love endures for ever.

HOLY THURSDAY

For the celebration of the triduum the focus of our prayer is the liturgy itself. Our prayer should build toward and prepare for the liturgy as well as flow from it. Each day we will provide a psalm which captures one of that day's themes and is appropriate for guiding our own prayer. And here we will point out some of the themes of the feast. This is not a commentary upon the liturgy so much as a highlighting of certain motifs.

The feast begins according to Jewish customs at sunset today. At the center of today's liturgy is our commemoration of Jesus' Last Supper with his disciples. And since that supper in turn is founded on the seder meal and passover we are immediately made aware of our Hebrew roots. The first passover celebrated the passing of the Lord over the first-born of Israel while the first-born of the Egyptians were slain. Here the blood of the lamb smeared upon the doorway signaled the angel of the Lord to pass over that house. John uses the image of the lamb to speak of Jesus. And in John's Gospel Jesus dies on the cross at the very time when the passover lambs are being slain in the temple in preparation for the feast.

But the passover is more than the seder supper, and our passover is more than the Lord's Supper. Israel went forth from the slavery of Egypt to pass over the Red Sea and eventually into the promised land. And Jesus passes over from death into resurrection and opens a promised land of eternal life to us.

Our pasch is also closely tied to the springtime. We celebrate on the first Sunday after the first full moon after the spring equinox. In the Hebrew passover we see the slaughter and feasting upon the new lamb—the first fruits of spring for a nomadic people. We see as well the instructions for baking the new bread without yeast. In the story this action commemorates the haste with which the Israelites had to leave Egypt. But it also reflects a springtime custom of throwing out the old year's yeast and beginning a new batch. The first breads would then be unleavened since the yeast is not yet ready.

The themes of spring bring a greater dimension to our Easter as well. In our Lent we have thrown out the stale and old yeast of our past life. We have repented and begun to live more from the yeast of the Gospel. Now we see the first fruits of that new yeast in Christ's passover. And while we celebrate the death and resurrection of Jesus, all around us are signs of new life and resurrection as the world greets the spring. Our ritual and our liturgy join us not simply with the great event of our salvation, but to our history and to our environment as well. We sense the unity of all creation.

Tonight we shall also celebrate the mandatum or foot washing. In John's Gospel at the Last Supper Jesus becomes a servant and washes his disciples' feet. Thus he provides a new model of leadership. The leader in the Christian community is the servant of all—not the ruler of all. The gesture of washing feet is quite powerful. We may have feelings of unworthiness such as Peter felt: "Lord, you will not wash my feet." And yet it is just these feelings that we need to deal with. In the mandatum we experience what Jesus has done for us, what he has given us already. And he tells us that if we would follow him, we must begin to act like him. The action of washing feet communicates this command as no words could do alone.

Tonight's liturgy concludes with the carrying of the Communion for tomorrow to the altar of repose. There is an inconclusiveness about this ending. For indeed we are not at the end, but have only begun our commemoration. Can we keep the spirit of these days not only in the liturgies we celebrate together but at other times as well? Tonight ends in quiet and repose. The silence invites us to prayer and meditation. We might want to keep vigil. We might also want to begin our fast. The earliest Christians fasted from the evening of Holy Thursday through the Vigil of Saturday. Our fasting could help us enter more deeply into the mysteries we celebrate these three days.

Psalm 133

How good and pleasant it is,
when brothers live in unity!

It is like precious oil upon the head
running down upon the beard,
running down upon Aaron's beard
upon the collar of his robes.

It is like the dew of Hermon which falls
on the heights of Zion.
For there the Lord gives his blessing,
life for ever.

FRIDAY OF HOLY WEEK

The image of the cross dominates this day. In today's liturgy, after the proclamation of the passion and our prayers, the cross is brought forward and all approach to venerate it. Here is one of the oldest symbols of humanity. The cross figure is found in every culture. It often represents opposites and reconciliation. In the cross two planes intersect—the vertical or heaven and the horizontal or earth. In Christianity we see the cross as the cruel inhuman instrument of Roman punishment, but at the same time we rejoice in it as the instrument of our salvation. And so it is with this Friday called Good. It is not simply the day of Jesus' death; it is the day on which our salvation is won.

In the liturgy today this theme of opposites permeates all. In the Song of the Servant from Isaiah the servant is rejected, scorned and brutalized. Yet by his stripes we are all healed. And we see past the grave to a new dawn when the servant shall justify many and when he shall be vindicated. In John's account of the passion, as we have seen, the Easter vision of Jesus is already breaking through. Here is no longer the Jesus who suffers agonies. Already he is the king of glory standing unrecognized before Pilate, but conscious of who he is and how already Pilate's days are at an end.

Some of the words of this service might give rise to unfortunate ideas, however. For in this liturgy even in its revised format there are many references to the Jews which are not flattering or commendable. This tension between Christians and Jews is part of our history and needs to be understood. In John's time the Christians had just been driven out of the synagogues—the rupture between the two groups is complete.

Besides, the Christians are suffering from Jewish persecution. John's use of the term "Jews" usually means not the Jewish people as a whole but rather the Jewish leaders who were antagonistic toward Jesus. But, sadly, the history of anti-Semitism from this time on finds fuel here. Furthermore the Romans seem to come off as almost nice guys. But these attitudes and ideas are part of the early Christian outlook created through persecution and rejection. As the Second Vatican Council finally proclaimed, the blame for Jesus' death cannot be laid on the Jewish people.

Indeed if we wish to be theologically correct we have to say that we are all responsible for Jesus' death—he died for sinners. When we hear references to the Jews in the Gospels we might take them as references to ourselves. We too are people of the promise who have failed to live up to our promise. This failure is no more appropriate to Israel than to all peoples, past and present. And we Christians should have much on our consciences for the centuries of anti-Semitism during which we maintained our "righteousness" by shifting the blame upon a scapegoat.

Indeed the image of the scapegoat is appropriate for us to reflect upon today. It comes from Israel's tradition. Once a year the villagers would gather together. A goat would be brought in and all the sins of the past year would be symbolically placed upon the goat. Then the goat was driven away into the desert to die, taking with it all the sins of the village. It is a beautiful image of the way in which we would like to absolve ourselves.

But Jesus never uses this image of the scapegoat for himself. Instead Christians identify him with the passover lamb. The lamb too takes upon itself the sins of the people. But the lamb is not driven away to be forgotten. Instead the lamb becomes the center of the feast—and all eat of it. Our sins are transformed. They come back to us, not to accuse us, but to nourish us, to heal us, to tell us of our salvation. Scapegoats allow us to shirk responsibility. But the lamb shows us our sins as well as what they might be changed into through the power and grace of God—the lamb offers us responsibility. We see not only who we are in sin but who we are called to become in Christ.

So it is with the cross as well. The Romans imposed it upon Jesus and others as a symbol of the worst human beings could do. God gives it back to us through Jesus as a symbol of the best God can do—reconciliation for estrangement and opposition, forgiveness instead of punishment, life and joy rather than pain and death.

Psalm 22

My God, my God, why have you forsaken me?
You are far from my plea and the cry of my distress.
O my God, I call by day and you give no reply.

Yes you, O God, are holy,
enthroned on the praises of Israel.
In you our fathers put their trust;
they trusted and you set them free.
When they cried to you, they escaped.
In you they trusted and never in vain.

But I am a worm and no person,
the butt of men, laughing-stock of the people.
All who see me deride me.
They curl their lips, they toss their heads.
He trusted in the Lord, let him save him;
let him release him if this is his friend.

Yes, it was you who took me from the womb,
entrusted me to my mother's breast.
To you I was committed from my birth,
from my mother's womb you have been my God.
Do not leave me alone in my distress;
come close, there is none else to help.

Many bulls have surrounded me,
fierce bulls of Bashan close me in.
Against me they open wide their jaws,
like lions, rending and roaring.

Like water I am poured out,
disjointed are all my bones.
My heart has become like wax,
it is melted within my breast.

Parched as burnt clay is my throat,
my tongue cleaves to my jaws.

Many dogs have surrounded me,
a band of the wicked beset me.
They tear holes in my hands and my feet
and lay me in the dust of death.

I can count every one of my bones.
These people stare at me and gloat;
they divide my clothing among them.
They cast lots for my robe.

O Lord, do not leave me alone,
my strength, make haste to help me!
Rescue my soul from the sword,
my life from the grip of these dogs.
Save my life from the jaws of these lions,
my poor soul from the horns of these oxen.

I will tell of your name to my brethren
and praise you where they are assembled.
"You who fear the Lord, give him praise;
all sons of Jacob, give him glory.
Revere him, Israel's sons.

For he has never despised
nor scorned the poverty of the poor.
From him he has not hidden his face,
but he heard the poor man when he cried."

You are my praise in the great assembly.
My vows I will pay before those who fear him.
The poor shall eat and shall have their fill.
They shall praise the Lord, those who seek him.
May their hearts live for ever and ever!

All the earth shall remember and return to the Lord,
all families of the nations worship before him,
for the kingdom is the Lord's; he is ruler of the nations.
They shall worship him, all the mighty of the earth;
before him shall bow all who go down to the dust.

And my soul shall live for him, my children serve him.
They shall tell of the Lord to generations yet to come,
declare his faithfulness to peoples yet unborn:
"These things the Lord has done."

SATURDAY OF HOLY WEEK

This is a day of waiting and praying. You might want to continue
your fast through today. After all it is appropriate that we fast
before we feast. But whatever you do, schedule this day for yourself
to prepare for your initiation.

You might review once more your journey toward faith. From this
special perspective what have been the major stepping-stones to

faith? What were the obstacles and how were they overcome? Can you see your journey differently now from the time when you were in the middle of things?

You might also look ahead to the future. How do you envision yourself a year fron now in terms of your faith? Are there certain activities you would like to become involved in? What would you hope for in this coming year in terms of your continuing spiritual growth?

But mostly today simply remain in quiet and silence. Take a walk in the woods. Go someplace beautiful and simply enjoy the present. It is a day for rest and doing nothing, but hardly a day on which nothing can happen.

Psalm 130

O Lord, my heart is not proud
nor haughty my eyes.
I have not gone after things too great
nor marvels beyond me.

Truly I have set my soul
in silence and peace.
A weaned child on its mother's breast,
even so is my soul.

O Israel, hope in the Lord
both now and for ever.

APPENDIX—PRAYER SERVICES

ASH WEDNESDAY—PRAYER SERVICE ON ELECTION

Prayer of petition: LORD, HEAR OUR PRAYER.

Psalm 61

O God, you are my God, for you I long;
for you my soul is thirsting.
My body pines for you
like a dry, weary land without water.
I gaze on you in the sanctuary
to see your strength and your glory.

For your love is better than life,
my lips will speak your praise.
So I will bless you all my life,
in your name I will lift up my hands.
My soul shall be filled as with a banquet,
my mouth shall praise you with joy.

On my bed I remember you
On you I muse through the night:
for you have been my help;
in the shadow of your wings I rejoice.
My soul clings to you;
your right hand holds me fast.

FIRST WEEK OF LENT—CONTEMPLATIVE PRAYER SERVICE

Responsorial Psalm: THE LORD IS KING, THE MOST HIGH OVER ALL THE EARTH.

Prayer of petition: LORD, SHOW US THE FATHER, AND WE SHALL BE SATISFIED.

Psalm 82

How lovely is your dwelling place,
Lord, God of hosts.

My soul is longing and yearning,
is yearning for the courts of the Lord.
My heart and my soul ring out their joy
to God, the living God.

The sparrow herself finds a home
and the swallow a nest for her brood;
she lays her young by your altars,
Lord of hosts, my king and my God.

They are happy, who dwell in your house,
for ever singing your praise.
They are happy, whose strength is in you,
in whose hearts are the roads to Zion.

As they go through the Bitter Valley
they make it a place of springs,
the autumn rain covers it with blessings.
They walk with ever growing strength,
they will see the God of gods in Zion.

O Lord God of hosts, hear my prayer,
give ear, O God of Jacob.

Turn your eyes, O God, our shield,
look on the face of your anointed.

One day within your courts
is better than a thousand elsewhere.
The threshold of the house of God
I prefer to the dwellings of the wicked.

For the Lord God is a rampart, a shield;
he will give us his favor and glory.
The Lord will not refuse any good
to those who walk without blame.

Lord, God of hosts,
happy the man who trusts in you!

SECOND WEEK OF LENT—SERVICE OF SCRIPTURE READING

A reading from the Gospel according to John (Jn 3:1 - 21)

Now there was a man of the Pharisees,
named Nicodemus, a ruler of the Jews.

This man came to Jesus by night and said to him,
"Rabbi, we know that you are a teacher come from God;
for no one can do these signs that you do,
unless God is with him."

Jesus answered him,

"Truly, truly I say to you,
unless one is born anew, he cannot see the kingdom of God."

Nicodemus said to him,

"How can a man be born when he is old?
Can he enter a second time into his mother's womb and be born?"

Jesus answered,

"Truly, truly I say to you,
unless one is born of water and the Spirit,
he cannot enter the kingdom of God.

That which is born of the flesh is flesh,
and that which is born of the Spirit is spirit.

Do not marvel that I said to you, 'You must be born anew'.

The wind blows where it wills, and you hear the sound of it,
but you do not know whence it comes or whither it goes;
so it is with everyone who is born of the Spirit."

Nicodemus said to him,

"How can this be?"

Jesus answered him,

"Are you a teacher of Israel,
and yet you do not understand this?

Truly, truly, I say to you,
we speak of what we know, and bear witness to what we have seen;

If I have told you earthly things and you do not believe,
how can you believe if I tell you heavenly things?

No one has ascended into heaven but he who descended from

heaven,
the Son of man.

And as Moses lifted up the serpent in the wilderness,
so must the Son of man be lifted up,
that whoever believes in him may have eternal life."

For God so loved the world that he gave his only Son,
that whoever believes in him should not perish but have eternal life.

For God sent the Son into the world, not to condemn the world,
but that the world might be saved through him.

He who believes in him is not condemned;
he who does not believe is condemned already,
because he has not believed in the name of the only Son of God.

And this is the judgment,
that the light has come into the world,
and men loved darkness rather than light,
because their deeds were evil.

For every one who does evil hates the light,
and does not come to the light,
lest his deeds should be exposed.

But he who does what is true comes to the light,
that it may be clearly seen
that his deeds have been wrought in God.

Prayer of petition: LORD HEAR OUR PRAYER.

Psalm 119:105 - 112

Your word is a lamp for my steps
and a light for my path.
I have sworn and have made up my mind
to obey your decrees.
Lord, I am deeply afflicted:
by your word give me life.
Accept, Lord, the homage of my lips
and teach me your decrees.
Though I carry my life in my hands,
I remember your law.
Though the wicked try to ensnare me
I do not stray from your precepts.
Your will is my heritage for ever,
the joy of my heart.
I set myself to carry out your statutes
in fullness, for ever.

THIRD WEEK OF LENT—PRESENTATION OF THE CREED

Responsorial psalm: LORD, YOU HAVE THE WORDS OF ETERNAL LIFE

The Nicene-Constantinople Creed

We believe in one God,
the Father, the Almighty,
maker of heaven and earth,
of all that is seen and unseen.

We believe in one Lord, Jesus Christ,
the only Son of God,
eternally begotten of the Father,

God from God, Light from Light,
true God from true God,
begotten, not made, one in Being with the Father.
Through him all things were made.
For us men and for our salvation
he came down from heaven:
by the power of the Holy Spirit
he was born of the Virgin Mary,
and became man.

For our sake he was crucified under Pontius Pilate:
he suffered, died, and was buried.
On the third day he rose again,
in fulfillment of the Scriptures;
he ascended into heaven
and is seated at the right hand of the Father.

He will come again in glory to judge the living and the dead,
and his kingdom will have no end.

We believe in the Holy Spirit, the Lord, the giver of life,
who proceeds from the Father and the Son.

With the Father and the Son he is worshiped and glorified.
He has spoken through the prophets.

We believe in one holy catholic and apostolic Church,

We acknowledge one baptism for the forgiveness of sins.

We look for the resurrection of the dead,
and the life of the world to come. Amen.

Prayer of petition: WE BELIEVE, O LORD.

FOURTH WEEK OF LENT—THE HEALING OF MEMORIES

Responsorial psalm: O LORD, RESTORE ME TO HEALTH AND MAKE ME LIVE!
Prayer of petition: HEAL US, LORD!

Psalm 122

To you have I lifted up my eyes,
you who dwell in the heavens:
my eyes, like the eyes of slaves
on the hand of their lords.

Like the eyes of a servant
on the hand of her mistress,
so our eyes are on the Lord our God
till he show us his mercy.

Have mercy on us, Lord, have mercy.
We are filled with contempt.
Indeed all too full is our soul
with the scorn of the rich,
with the proud man's disdain.

FIFTH WEEK OF LENT—PRESENTATION OF THE LORD'S PRAYER

Psalm 23

The Lord is my shepherd;
there is nothing I shall want.
Fresh and green are the pastures
where he gives me repose.
Near restful waters he leads me,
to revive my drooping spirit.

He guides me along the right path;
he is true to his name.
If I should walk in the valley of darkness
no evil would I fear.
You are there with your crook and your staff;
with these you give me comfort.

You have prepared a banquet for me
in the sight of my foes.
My head you have anointed with oil;
my cup is overflowing.

Surely goodness and kindness shall follow me
all the days of my life.
In the Lord's own house shall I dwell
for ever and ever.

Prayer of petition: GIVE US THIS DAY OUR DAILY BREAD.

The Lord's Prayer

Our Father,
who art in heaven.

Hallowed be thy name.
Thy kingdom come.
Thy will be done,
on earth as it is in heaven.

Give us this day our daily bread;
And forgive us our trespasses,
as we forgive those who trespass against us;

And lead us not into temptation,
but deliver us from evil.